I Thank Therefore I Am

I Thank Therefore I Am

Gratefulness As Healing

Henry Glazer

Copyright © 2008 by Henry Glazer.

ISBN: Softcover   978-1-4363-7701-0

All rights reserved. No part of this book may be reproduced or transmitted in any form or by any means, electronic or mechanical, including photocopying, recording, or by any information storage and retrieval system, without permission in writing from the copyright owner.

This is a work of fiction. Names, characters, places and incidents either are the product of the author's imagination or are used fictitiously, and any resemblance to any actual persons, living or dead, events, or locales is entirely coincidental.

This book was printed in the United States of America.

To order additional copies of this book, contact:
Xlibris Corporation
1-888-795-4274
www.Xlibris.com
Orders@Xlibris.com
54336

CONTENTS

INTRODUCTION..11

PART ONE

CHAPTER 1: *GRATEFULNESS—WHAT DOES IT MEAN?*..........23
CHAPTER 2: *FROM GRIPING TO GRATEFULNESS* 31
CHAPTER 3: *FROM GREED TO GRATEFULNESS*......................37
CHAPTER 4: *FROM GUILT TO GRATEFULNESS*........................40
CHAPTER 5: *FROM GRANDIOSITY TO GRATEFULNESS* 46
CHAPTER 6: *FROM GRIEF TO GRATEFULNESS* 52

PART TWO

CHAPTER 7: *EXISTENCE AS GRATEFULNESS:*
"I AM THEREFORE I THANK"................................61
CHAPTER 8: *GRATEFULNESS AND SELF* 65
CHAPTER 9: *EVIL AND GRATEFULNESS*...................................72
CHAPTER 10: *GRATEFULNESS-A UNIVERSAL GIFT* 86

    CHRISTIANITY..87
    ISLAM..88
    BUDDHISM...90
    SECULARISM 92

CHAPTER 11: *MAKING GRATEFULNESS A PART OF YOUR LIFE: A JEWISH APPROACH* 95

    1. TORAH-AWARENESS 95
    2. AVODAH-WORSHIP 103
    3. GEMILUT CHASSADIM-COMPASSION 113

CHAPTER 12: *FROM GRATEFULNESS TO LOVE* 114
CHAPTER 13: *GRATEFULNESS AND THE FAMILY: THE FAMILY GRATEFUL TOGETHER, STAYS TOGETHER*...............................120
CHAPTER 14: *GOD AND GRATEFULNESS* 126
CHAPTER 15: *SOME PERSONAL AFTERTHOUGHTS*................131
CHAPTER 16: *MORE GRATEFULNESS MEDITATIONS* 134

ENDNOTES 141

With gratitude to my parents
                for their gift of life,
                love and decency.

ACKNOWLEDGEMENTS:

Words cannot fully capture the depth of my thanks. Yet, words are all I have for this space.

First, I wish to extend warmest gratitude to my spiritual teachers at Éylat Hayyim, Sylvia, Boorstein, Rabbi Sheila Pelz Weinberger and Rabbi Jeff Roth.

I am blessed with a unique spiritual mentor in the person of Dr. David Aftergood, psychiatrist, teacher and a genuine "mensch."

When I first began to write, I presented several individuals with a manuscript that was more a jungle than a well-cultivated field of cohesive and readable writing.

A colleague and able editor, Rabbi Stephan Parnes, generously took the type written manuscript and patiently and gently encouraged me to make the multitude of changes necessary to convert this jumble of ideas into something approaching a workable manuscript.

Ethan Elenberg and Al Zuckerman, both highly successful literary agents, provided invaluable assistance and guidance.

My good friend, Ira Rifkin, a seasoned journalist and writer of several books on the impact of globalization on spiritual life, firmly continued to lead me along the path of greater refinement and clarity in presenting my words on paper.

Finally, I had the exceptional good fortune to find Sarah Van Arsdale, a wonderful fiction writer, editor and human being, who insightfully and compassionately took me to the finish line of the track along which I jogged.

My deepest gratitude is reserved for my family. My daughter Jessica, with great care and wisdom read my manuscript and suggested changes and corrections that only a sensitive soul such as hers can arrive at. My son

Jeremiah was always ready to engage in philosophical dialogue by which I could better clarify my thinking.

And my wife Rose, my spiritual mentor for thirty years, 'at aleet al koolanah'—you surpass them all.

To the Source of All things—the Creator and Compassionate Giver of Life—to whom I try to offer my life with growing gratefulness, I remain as always, grateful for this gift of having written the enclosed words. "Shehecheyanu V'keeyemanu"-I thank God for sustaining me to reach this day. Amen

INTRODUCTION

For the blessings which You lavish upon us

In forest and sea, in mountain and meadow,
In rain and in sun, we thank You.

For the blessings You implant within us,

Joy and peace, meditation and laughter,
We are grateful to You

For the blessings of friendship and love
Of family and community,

For the blessings we ask of You
And those we cannot ask,

For the blessings You bestow upon us openly
And those You give us in secret,

For all those blessings, Lord,
We thank You and are grateful to You.

For the blessings we recognize
And those we fail to recognize,

For the blessings of our tradition
And our holy days,

For the blessings of return and forgiveness
Of memory, of vision, and of hope—

For all these blessings which surround us on every side
Dear God,
Hear our thanks and accept our gratitude."[1]

—Ruth Brin

I was buying flowers for my wife in honor of Mother's Day. Waiting for the salesperson to wrap the flowers, I glanced around my favorite food store, relishing the sights and smells of these luscious surroundings. I spotted a group of cards available to customers on which to register comments and suggestions. These letters were emblazoned at the top: **RANTS & RAVES.** It occurred to me that this invitation extended beyond an immediate response to the service or quality of the food available in this store. In fact it could embrace our attitude to the totality of life. Do we rant at life or rave about it? Do we grumble and carry on unhappily, or can we discover the grace and strength by which to relate to all things gratefully and joyfully? This is a choice that confronts us each moment of our lives. It is this choice that is the subject of the following work.

Gratefulness is pivotal to the spiritual enrichment of our lives. Its source is contained in the great spiritual traditions of the world-Judaism, Christianity, Islam, Buddhism, and the secular "new-age" ideologies that are quite prevalent today.

Gratefulness is so important that its absence, ingratitude, was considered a disastrous moral failing in the opinions of prominent Western philosophers and in the writings of playwrights and thinkers. David Hume is quite forceful when he states: "Of all crimes that human creatures are capable of committing, the most horrid and unnatural is ingratitude . . ."[2] Immanuel Kant, the great 18th century German philosopher declared ingratitude "one of the most detestable vices."[3] Shakespeare has King Lear announce

> *Ingratitude, thou marble-hearted fiend,*
> *More hideous when thou showest thee in a child*
> *Than the sea-monster.*

In Twelfth Night (III 4 390) Shakespeare tell us:

> *I hate ingratitude more in a man*
> *Than lying, vainness, babbling, drunkenness,*
> *Or any taint of vice whose strong corruption*
> *Inhabits our frail blood.*

One could surmise, therefore, that gratefulness would be considered a paramount virtue to be pursued and cultivated with ardor and dedication. Yet, as an aspect of study and careful consideration, gratefulness has received very little attention during the last half of the twentieth century.

When written about, it has received only superficial attention and continues to remain disconnected from the inner lives of most people. Some maintain that while the idea of gratefulness is popular, "it is one of the most underestimated of the virtues, and even in broad surveys of attitudes, it is often ignored."[4] We pay lip service to the significance of being grateful and why it is a necessary part of being a mature and a decent, moral human being. We teach our young to say thank you when receiving a gift or favor, and consider the neglect of such etiquette or protocol a failure of character and upbringing. But the deeper impact of gratefulness on our lives, its transformative power as a means of greater well-being and happiness, is lost or ignored.

I will address some of the reasons for this widespread phenomenon and consider the psychological, moral and historical obstacles that stand in the way of achieving a more fully developed sense of gratefulness in our lives.

In this book, I explore this spiritual dynamic comprehensively, examining its rich contours and content from the perspectives of my personal experience and the tradition I am committed to, the views and considerations of Judaism. Moreover, a chapter is devoted to the centrality of gratefulness in the worldviews of other major religious outlooks and from the point of view of secular thinking as well. The exercises provided, as guides to translating this concept into everyday living are universal in focus and address the life experiences of a broad range of people. Also, I am persuaded that the more particular approach of Judaism has relevant application to the belief systems of other faith communities as well. Since all theistic religions encompass prayer to a deity, the study of a sacred scripture and the performance of compassionate acts, Judaism's message and approach will resonate with responses that can be applied to all faith communities.

Beyond the general, conceptual and intellectual references to gratefulness as the linchpin of spiritual life, I flesh out the phenomenon of gratefulness in philosophical, psychological and spiritual terms so as to share with the reader a firmer grasp of the idea with the hope that she/he incorporate it into her/his life as an instrument for personal spiritual transformation. I have included concrete exercises at the end of most chapters and some additional suggestions for meditation as a final chapter in an attempt to facilitate the process of cultivating gratefulness. The reader is encouraged to engage the senses-touch, smell, sight, hearing and taste—as avenues of greater gratefulness awareness. For those who find it natural and comfortable to express themselves in writing, a "gratefulness journal" is recommended. A more all-encompassing vehicle by which to record and remember moments of gratefulness is the "scrap book," a resource that can readily be used to collect not only writings but items that are connections to happy and rewarding experiences in one's life such as photographs, mementos, documents and sundry other data. If you are religiously inclined, you may entitle your journal "my Blessing journal"; moreover, your prayers can become powerful instruments for enhanced gratefulness consciousness.

More specific and detailed extensions of these general approaches will be made available further on in the book.

A comment from a gratitude "blog" tells the following anecdote.

"When my sister was in kindergarten their class had a Moral Science course. During a session on gratitude, the teacher handed all the kids a list of things and asked them to circle those things they were grateful for.

After circling home, food, mother, father etc. they came to "brother." One child wondered aloud exclaiming; "I can't be grateful for a brother. I don't have a brother."

"Circle it," my sister said. "You should be grateful."

I believe that gratefulness can serve as the spiritual foundation of a new ethic that can resonate more authentically in our lives and can make an indelibly transforming impact on our everyday lives in general, in our families, in our schools, and certainly in our houses of worship.

A "gratefulness" turning point in my life was unexpectedly arrived at during a meditation retreat at *Elat Chayyim*, a Center for Jewish Spirituality in Connecticut. The five day retreat was designed for rabbis and other leaders of the Jewish community to engage them in the spiritual approach of mindfulness meditation. Each day was devoted entirely to sitting and walking meditations and was spent in silence (no easy task for a group of rabbis) during which participants had no contact with the outside world. The only exception was to address questions of clarification to our teachers and to articulate concerns during individual mentoring evaluations.

It was the third night of the retreat. I was unable to sleep; I was restless with numbness—my heart and mind were blocked of any genuine emotion and connection. All I could sense was the emptiness of isolation. In the middle of the night, not having slept, I made my way into the cool night and began to jog. It was a moonless night and it felt as if I were running on faith, unable to see much of the road ahead of me. Yet, I persisted to push my way into the dark cold night air. About a half hour had elapsed and I gratefully began to feel fatigue floating into my body. I headed back to the sleeping quarters, and was graced with the gift of several hours of restful sleep.

That morning, during the day's first sitting meditation, I focused upon the first Jewish prayer in the morning upon awakening, "*Modeh Ani*"—"I thank you" (for waking up another morning). I then proceeded to recite the formal morning prayers wearing the *Tallit* (Prayer shawl) and *Tefillin* (phylacteries). I stepped over to a corner of the large meditation room, placed the prayer shawl over my head, and suddenly, without warning, was gripped by a torrent of uncontrolled sobbing. It was as if floodgates of feeling that had been dammed up in my heart had suddenly burst open and for what seemed like an eternity, my body heaved with the eruption of tears and feelings that seemed to have sprung from the deepest wellsprings of my soul. I couldn't stop. As I wept, all I could feel was the sensation of being thankful, and I repeated to myself, over and over again, "thank you, thank you God",—"*Modeh Ani lefanehcha*"—"I am thankful before You".

There was nothing specific for which I was grateful—simply for being alive, for being blessed with a heart that was finally open and receptive to feeling fully alive and fully conscious, that somewhere there was something, something intimate and indispensable for the fullness of my life, something to which or to whom I was profoundly grateful.

This time the words of the prayer became a living, genuine reality. No matter how brief, transient and temporary it was, in those few moments, I understood the meaning of prayer.

This was my experience of the words of the Buddhist teacher, Ajahn Chah who once said: "If you haven't wept deeply, you haven't begun to meditate."[5]

I had lived almost all my life—or to be more accurate, a significant part of my inner life—hampered by an unrelenting inability to feel gratefulness for the many blessings that have been showered upon me.

I have struggled psychologically and spiritually to sever that chain of inner enslavement. It's only a matter of a few years since I have succeeded in arriving at an increasing awareness that gratefulness is in fact indispensable for one's sense of freedom and happiness. Its discovery within us is a necessary prerequisite for a meaningful and moral life.

Many hours spent in an analyst's office, and in study, prayer and thought have contributed to my emerging awareness about gratefulness and its centrality in life, without which I could never have entertained writing this book. At the same time, inner obstacles and impasses have forced me to re-evaluate, re-examine, and re-discover truths, which, while embedded in my religious and spiritual tradition, I was unable to fully recognize. I was so enmeshed in the negative and problematic aspects of religion that its enriching and life-affirming qualities escaped me.

My relationship to Judaism expressed itself professionally—I became a rabbi-, but personally it was permeated with a sense of guilt and fear. For me, associated with things Jewish was the fear of failure, fear of disapproval and rejection, fear of being found wanting and incomplete, fear of being unloved, and a great deal of guilt, especially that associated with the eruption of teenage sexual feelings and obsessive erotic thoughts. While Judaism afforded me a special identity, it also assumed a reality that was onerous and burdensome. There was little actual joy and inspiration in a deep and personally meaningful way. All the wonderful and wise words, rituals, ideas and values of Judaism were mine only in an intellectually superficial manner, and were unable to find their way to where they belonged, in my heart and soul. The language of God seemed so far away, "up in the heavens and across the sea,"[6] never within the grasp of my gut, my inner world of truth.

Even today, I often have to repeatedly resist deeply ingrained patterns of ingratitude and dissatisfaction, and with disciplined effort, reach out to the horizon of greater gratitude and the awareness of life's blessing that "Is very close to you, in your mouth and in your heart, to observe it."[7]

If I were to pinpoint a starting point of my personal spiritual journey it would be at my becoming a Bar Mitzvah fifty-four years ago. This journey, of course, cannot be precisely fixed at a particular moment in time. The soul unfolds in an amorphous and dynamic way. Many processes began earlier in my life

Around the age of my Bar Mitzvah, I fell into a psychological trap of the following misguided equation: "I am intelligent, therefore I am!" I invested my identity and well being on the foundation of "being smart." I made a deal with God. If He would endow me with "intelligence," I would become an avid servant of His by following all the precepts of Judaism in an orthodox manner.

Like many immigrant families, my family put a premium on intelligence and education. Formal schooling would rescue us from the shackles of menial work. For my brother, like his successful uncle (my father's only educated brother among six siblings), the law would lead to money and success. For me, religion would enrich my life not with wealth but with the prestige of rabbinic status and recognition.

In my family, a myth pervaded our emotional lives based on the following assumption: had my father been allowed to pursue a singing career, all of us would have been financially comfortable, highly respected and ultimately happy. Instead, due to family pressures after my grandfather passed on, my father was obligated to abandon his singing lessons and take his father's place in the family's butcher business. As a result, my mother, Rose, in subtle and not so subtle ways, transmitted to her family an unrelenting anger and dissatisfaction over being cheated of our family birthright and all the privileges and benefits she assumed went with it.

Perhaps unwittingly and unconsciously, she believed that by remaining ungrateful she could hold on to a fantasy that one day her missed opportunities for greater happiness and success would become a reality. If she suffered enough, somehow she would eventually be rewarded. She was not prepared to risk the loss of that dream by giving it up and feeling grateful for a reality that fell short of what she felt she deserved.

By contrast, my father, Joseph, enjoyed the simple joys of life and rarely, if ever, complained about anything. He was in fact a very grateful man, worked hard, cared for his family and was sincerely thankful for the basic gifts of health, home, family and the opportunity to sing at family celebrations and in synagogue choirs on the High Holydays. His failure to pursue a singing career never embittered him.

Somehow I appropriated my mother's attitude of dogged ungratefulness. My mother's forceful presence imposed itself on her three children so that each one of us felt the obligation to compensate for her unhappiness and lack of fulfillment. My father, meanwhile, took a back seat in the emotional configuration of the family. My mother's voice was obviously a little louder than that of my father.

Because my emotional life was so punctuated with fear and uncertainty, my life unfolded so that its essence coalesced around the pursuit of God via the examination of religion and philosophy, and at the same time through a process of on-going self-examination in the offices of the analyst and psychotherapist.

Being Jewish in a traditional manner was not alien to me or to my family. As a pre-teen, I fell in love with Judaism as a result of an adoring and humble Orthodox *zeide*, my mother's father, and the enthusiasm generated by two Hebrew school teachers in particular, who together succeeded in imparting to me a genuine love of and commitment to the Jewish people and Judaism as a serious way of life.

Becoming a rabbi was an inescapable necessity for my personal identity and survival. Not only would I persevere to achieve perfection as a Jew, but also I would devote my life to persuading others to do the same. In this way, I would leave God no choice but to bless me with the fulfillment of my desired goal—to be smarter than my friend Yossie and more capable than the rabbi of my youth whom I had idealized.

These feelings simmered inside me, forming a psychological barrier, a dam that blocked the natural flow of gratefulness and joy that otherwise would have bubbled up to the surface and blessed my life.

I've had good health, success, a wonderful family, and the privilege of living in a country of opportunity and peace.

Nevertheless, to me the cup was never half full. I found myself constantly focusing on the half empty part of the cup, screaming inside in protest at God—why isn't my cup fuller, as full as this one or that one, people who of course were less deserving than I was. My cry heavenward was infused with righteous indignation, convinced that my life was of greater moral and religious propriety than others who did enjoy success and happiness!

I am continuously challenged to recognize these feelings, to place them in a realistic context and then proceed to rise above them and arrive at a different psychic reality. I do this through a conscious, meditative process, reaching inward to attain greater awareness of the giftedness of life and the accompanying encounter with gratefulness.

My daily life is now suffused with prayer that helps me to be ever mindful of a God as Giver and the source of gratefulness as the ultimate spiritual realization in my life. In the quiet of everyday, ordinary thinking and musing, and in the course of formal prescribed Jewish prayer, I make a concerted effort to be as mindful as I can of the staggering diversity of gifts that envelops my every moment of life.

All of us are confronted with the existential reality of our lives as being brief, without any logical explanation and potentially a source of meaninglessness and futility, so brilliantly understood by the author of the book of Ecclesiastes. To serve a higher goal, however, with an openness of heart and gratefulness, is a meaningful choice that may allow for encountering life with an attitude of faith, purpose and well-being.

When I retired from a full-time pulpit position, I stepped into the transition between a steady job with a permanent and clearly defined place in the community to an occupational setting that was fluid and undefined, my anxiety was intensified and exacerbated by something more basic to who I am. What would Judaism mean to me now? I would now have to examine my religious ideology and way of life dismantled of its professional accoutrements and the public face that it used to wear. How would I live up to the demands of Judaism without the scrutiny of the synagogue? My struggle for an authentic spiritual identity, begun earlier in my life despite the practical considerations of job and family, would now be undertaken with even greater earnestness and commitment.

That day, ten years ago, at Elat Chayyim, my *talit*, my prayer shawl, was wet. I could taste the salty sweat and tears that had seeped into the fibers of the woolen garment. I wiped away my tears, looked up and noticed my fellow meditators seated once again preparing to connect with their souls. I returned to the group as my heart returned to its earlier status of being shut and the freshness and spiritual impact of this special "peace" experience faded and waned. I realized then that like all things in life, which are essentially impermanent, each and every experience not only passes with time but loses its fullness and vitality as well. All we can do is to try to remember, in a mindful and meaningful way, so that the flickering embers of a once blazing flame can be nursed and tended allowing some glimmer of light to continue to glow gently in the darkness of our lives. This I must do with gratefulness.

PART ONE

CHAPTER 1

GRATEFULNESS—WHAT DOES IT MEAN?

"Have you ever seen
Anything
In your life
More wonderful

Than the way the sun,
Every evening
Relaxed and easy
Floats toward the horizon

And into the clouds or the hills
Or the rumpled sea,
And is gone—
And how it slides again

Out of the blackness
Every morning,
On the other side of the world
Like a
Red flower
Streaming upwards on its heavenly oils,
Say, on a morning in early summer,
At its perfect imperial distance—
And have you felt for anything

Such wild love—
Do you think there is anywhere, in any language?
A word billowing enough
For the pleasure
That fills you
As the sun
Reaches out,
As it warms you—
As you stand there
Empty handed—
Or have you too turned from this world-

Or have you too
Gone crazy,
For power for things?"[8]

—Mary Oliver

Language has great power. On a macro level it molds civilizations. On a micro level it shapes our perceptions of the world and our reaction to the events of the day. According to Bennet and Hacker in *Philosophical Foundations of Neuroscience*, "Possession of a language broadens the range of possible emotional responses no less than it widens the horizon of thought and will. It makes possible not only reflection on the world we encounter around us, but also on our own responses, cognitive and affective, to what we thus find."[9]

In common usage, "gratefulness" and "gratitude"—which derive from a common Latin root—*gratia* or *gratus*—are often used interchangeably. I prefer to use "gratefulness" because the suffix *ful* conveys a greater sense of the fullness of the experience. It evokes a more all-embracing condition of being in a state of thankfulness and appreciation. A well-known Christian devotional writer, Benedictine monk and psychologist David Steindel-Rast, frames the concept this way. "Gratefulness" or "great fullness" is the full response of the human heart to the gratuitousness of all that is ... Personal gratitude deserves to be called *thankfulness,* because it typically expresses itself in thanks given to a giver by the receiver of the gift. Transpersonal gratitude deserves to be called *gratefulness,* because it is typically the full response of a person to gratuitous belonging."[10] Put succinctly, "gratefulness" expresses thanks for the most basic of gifts:" I am therefore I thank."

The dictionary definition of gratefulness is associated with *grates*, which means, "free, pleasing."[11] We are given life without doing anything, without deserving it, without having to struggle for it. It is free, a pure gift. Life is unexpected; it comes as a surprise. It is not frightening or worrisome but rather a source of anticipation, excitement and wonderment. Viewed this way, life can become an endless source of gratefulness.

The Hebrew word for "gratefulness" is *hakarat hatov*, which can be translated as the "the recognition of a favor." I would submit that this term has another definition that is highly germane to our topic. In Hebrew, *lehakir*, the infinitive form of *hakarat,* "to recognize," can also mean to "make the acquaintance of" someone or something. *Tov* can mean "favor" or "goodness." The power of gratefulness lies in its capacity to allow us to become emotionally and spiritually acquainted with the reality that all things, in some profound if not entirely observable way, are intrinsically—good. To be grateful is to see life as a constant source of goodness with which all people can make a warmer and more honest acquaintance.

"The dead cannot praise God, neither can those who descend to the Netherworld, the Place of silence. We, (who are alive) however, shall praise (bless) God now and Forever."[12]

From the standpoint of the above passage from Psalms, death can be viewed as a state of non-existence because the capacity, and the privilege, to praise, to articulate the experience of gratefulness no longer exists. In the thinking of the Psalmist, to be alive is to be in a spiritual position to praise, to recognize the gratefulness inherent in living without which life is incomplete, falling short of its potential fullness and losing its energy and vitality. [13]The thread of life is in fact gratefulness, without which life, in its deepest levels of spiritual and psychological meaning, can unravel into chaotic strands of confusion, dissatisfaction, greed and hostility.

The world-to-come like wise is permeated with the effusion of gratefulness. While no one knows for certain what transpires in the after-life, if in fact one exists, our tradition exercised its insightful imagination and understood this eventuality in the spirit of gratefulness and thanksgiving. "In the world to come all prayers will be eliminated except for prayers of thanksgiving which will never be abolished."[14] Life in this world and the next cannot be fulfilled unless it abounds in praise and thanksgiving. The very spiritual essence of life, one that is everlasting and ongoing, is the dynamic quality of gratefulness in the presence of the great gift of life.

Toward the end of the traditional Jewish morning prayers we recite: "May it be Your will, Lord our God and God of our ancestors, that we may observe your decrees in this world and merit that we live . . . And inherit goodness and blessing . . . in the life of the world to come, so that my soul might sing to you . . . Forever will I thank You!"[15]

This liturgical text provides us with a closer understanding of the nature of enjoying God's radiance in terms that are comprehensible and reflect a reality of this world. "So that my soul might sing to you . . . forever will I thank You!"[16] Gratefulness and the song of praise that flows from this awareness are the eternal essence of all of life, both in this world and the next.

When expounding on the long litany of "curses" which are the consequence of disobedience, the Torah itself makes the astounding declaration that a fundamental source of these most ominous and grim phenomena is the absence of gratefulness and a sense of joy that accompanies such gratefulness:

> —"All these curses shall befall you, they shall pursue you and overtake you and wipe you out . . . they shall serve as signs and

proofs against you and our offspring for all time because you would not serve the Lord your God in joy and gladness over the abundance of everything."[17]

From a practical and pragmatic point of view, studies have been conducted regarding the personal benefits of the cultivation of this virtue of gratefulness. According to Sharon Huffman, "feelings of gratitude release positive endorphins throughout the body, creating health." The release of endorphins into the body strengthen and enhance the immune system and stimulate the dilation of the blood vessels which can lead to a more relaxed and less stressed heart.

Michael E. McCullough, professor of psychology at the university of Miami and Prof. Robert Emmons of the University of California, Davis, were curious about why people involved in their faith seem to have more happiness and a greater sense of well-being than those who aren't. They conducted the Research Project on Gratitude and Thanksgiving. The study required several hundred people in three different groups to keep daily diaries. The first group kept a diary of all the events that occurred during the day, while the second group recorded their unpleasant experiences only. The last group made a daily list of things for which they were grateful.

The results of the study indicated that daily gratitude exercises resulted in higher levels of alertness, enthusiasm, determination, optimism and energy. Additionally, the gratitude group experienced less depression and stress, exercised more regularly, made more progress toward personal goals, and was more compassionate toward others.

The study also found that people who feel grateful are also more likely to feel loved. McCullough and Emmons also noted that gratitude encouraged a positive cycle of reciprocal kindness among people since one act of gratitude encourages another.[18]

These results also seem to show that gratitude works independently of religious attachment. Though gratitude is a substantial part of most religions, benefits extend to the general population, regardless of religious faith or lack thereof.

The social benefits of gratefulness are eminently obvious. Would you not prefer the company of someone who is grateful to one who carps and complains? For the sheer pleasure of social interaction, gratefulness is the glue of cohesion and joyful human intercourse. From an ordinary evening together with friends to a more formal or structured social setting, gratefulness promotes harmony and greater comfort. The converse, a climate of unhappiness and ingratitude, creates distance and alienation among people who desire human closeness and intimacy. Gratefulness elevates the spirit while its absence opens the door to unhappiness and despair. We all need to be recognized and appreciated, to feel that friends and loved ones are made happy by our presence. If confronted by people who are ungrateful, does this not leave us with a sense of being emotionally ignored if not actually violated?

Science too is a powerful avenue to enhanced awareness of the wonder and amazement of the world and life, which imbues the human spirit with a deep sense of gratefulness. Brian Greene, a professor of physics at Columbia University, made the following astute comments in a recent article in the New York Times-Week In Review section-Sunday June 1, 2008: "Science is a way of life. Science is a perspective. Science is a process that takes us from confusion to understanding . . . a transformation . . . a language of hope and inspiration . . . it's the birthright of every child, it's a necessity for every adult to look out on the world . . . and see that the wonder of the cosmos transcends everything that divides us."[19]

Spiritually and religiously, gratefulness is the bridge that can span the chasm between transient, mortal man and infinite immortal Divinity; it is a gateway to the Divine. Christopher Fry called it "exploration of God."

The Bible, in the voice of the prophet Micha, enjoins us to "Walk in God's ways . . ."[20] I would submit that to walk in God's ways, to emulate God, to pay God the highest compliment, is to become a giver as God is a Giver. In this way, gratefulness creates the climate for compassion, which can shed some light on the dark and shadowy spots of evil in this world.

The Psalmist declared: *"Va'ani Bechasdecha batachti, yageil libi beyeshuatehcha, ashirah La'adonai, ki gamalalai"*—I have trusted in Your love, I will rejoice in Your saving power, I will sing to the Lord, for He has been bountiful to me.[21] These words represent the essence of a mature and in-depth theology that resides at the very core of the thousand upon thousands of words that constitute Jewish liturgy and the prayer book. "*Va Ani*"—"And I"—I am me because of God's "chessed", love, generosity and kindness. God's love—compassion—is the source of all things, all the gifts of life in their totality, without the recognition of which my sense of self remains incomplete and immature.

The song or poetry of life is a product of awakening to its bounty, which is freely given by God; the gratefulness for it is the reason for my life and prayer.

From a more everyday, even prosaic and pragmatic point of view, gratefulness acts as a gauge of one's emotional and psychological well-being. If a day goes by during which a sense of gratefulness has been absent, something has been missing from the context of my internal life. Not thinking gratefully is a signal to me that I am either angry, depressed or unhappy about one thing or another. If that is the case, I consciously direct my mind to the wide scope of life's endless gifts for which I can and should feel grateful. Essentially, I focus on the basic reality of sheer existence, a reality that upon closer spiritual consideration is the most compelling reason for gratefulness. Our identities and our very existence are inexorably interconnected. Not only do I feel that "I thank, therefore I am" is an indispensable perception to human life but the converse," I am, therefore I thank" is also fundamental to the meaning of who we are and the wonder and mystery of human life.

"*Ki'gamal alai*"—not "*ki gamal li*"—suggests that God is not necessarily bountiful to me directly, the sense of directness reflected in the Hebrew word—"li"—but rather the text uses the word "alai", which literally can be translated as—"upon me", available to me, a bounty that awaits my taking hold of and for which I am expected to assume responsibility and share with others. I thank God for His blessings of insight and new-found understanding, and I trust that this feeling of gratefulness and this act of sharing will only enrich and enhance God's Presence in this world.

> *"There is joy*
> *In all:*
> *In the hair I brush each morning.*
> *In the Cannon towel, newly washed,*
> *That I rub my body with each morning,*
> *In the chapel of eggs I cook*
> *Each morning,*
> *In the outcry from the kettle*
> *That heats my coffee*
> *Each morning.*
> *In the spoon and the chair*
> *That cry 'hello there Anne'*
> *Each morning.*
> *In the godhead of the table*
> *That I set my silver, plate, cup upon*
> *Each morning*
> *All this is God.*
> *Right here in my pea-green house*

Each morning
And I mean,
Though often forget,
To give thanks,
To faint down by the kitchen table
In a prayer of rejoicing
As the holy birds at the kitchen window
Peck into their marriage of seeds.

So while I think of it,
Let me paint a thank-you on my palm
For this God, this laughter of the morning
Lest it go unspoken.
The joy that isn't shared, I've heard, dies young."[22]
—Anne Sexton

CHAPTER 2

FROM GRIPING TO GRATEFULNESS

"So after every case, you have to go up to somebody and say "thank you"? What a . . . nightmare."[23]

There is an old Yiddish saying that reads: "A chissoron, di kallah iz tsu shain." Translation: "A fault-finder complains even that the bride is too pretty." Our gripes and grumblings are louder than our expressions of gratefulness. Our clamoring seems to be persistent while our appreciation comes at widely separated moments. Psychiatrists' offices and the studies of clergy resonate with the persistent strains of faultfinding and ingratitude. Why? If the quality of gratefulness is so great a source of joy and fulfillment, why is it that so many find it beyond their grasp?

In a word, it's because of fear. These fears range from a fear of responsibility to the fear of being happy.

A common psychological dynamic that acts as a barrier to gratefulness is the propensity toward feelings of victimization which results in a litany of complaints. The fear of assuming a sense of independence and autonomy is such that individuals and groups prefer to experience feelings of being inadequate and victimized.

Groups that have suffered persecution often share a collective sense of victimization. For understandable reasons, given the long history of dispersion and discrimination culminating in the worst of all human horrors, the Holocaust, the dynamic of victimization is not uncommon among many Jews.

Even Jewish humor reflects this psychological orientation. A man boards a Chicago-bound train in Grand Central Station and sits down across from an old man reading a Yiddish newspaper. Half an hour later the man puts down his newspaper and starts to whine: "Oy, am I thirsty . . . . Oy, am I thirsty . . . . Oy, am I thirsty . . . ."

This goes on for a while and the other man, growing impatient with the complaints of the elderly gentleman, gets up and fetches him a cup of water from the water cooler at the end of the car. He stops in front of the old man and clears his throat. The old man looks up and drains the water from the cup. He sits back relieved and allows himself a sigh of thanks. He leans into his seat, tilts his head toward the ceiling and says, just as loudly as before. "Oy, was I thirsty . . . ."

In a recent book on the Yiddish language and its culture the author points out humorously yet poignantly that "kvetching", grumbling and complaining, suggests "a way of life that has nothing to do with the fulfillment or frustration of desire . . . . it is a way of knowing, a means of apprehension that sees the world through cataract-colored glasses."[24]

If we go back to Biblical times, ancient Israel, especially the generation of the wilderness, is portrayed as blind to God's gifts and blessings, incessantly griping to Moses and to God. The entire prophetic enterprise takes Israel to task for its waywardness, emphasizing time and time again the ingratitude and vanity of Israel's spiritual and moral life. Traditional commentators and scholars have ascribed Israel's religious immaturity and ingratitude to its harsh and prolonged experience of enslavement and persecution. It is no wonder that a people without a country for two thousand years, a minority in a hostile and hateful environment, should view themselves as vulnerable victims. "*Kvetching,* complaining, becomes a way of exercising some small measure of control over an otherwise hostile environment."[25]

Over the centuries, this victimization has become increasingly internalized, a psychology difficult to modify or eradicate. Even in current conditions of greater freedom and national independence, a visceral vestige of victimization persists. Perhaps, if we stop "kvetching" and stop feeling ourselves as victims, we fear, we will forget who we really are. After all, in a convoluted way, as long as we grumble we remind ourselves of how special we are.

A sense of powerlessness is shared by everyone today. The world is gripped by uncertainty, as we head toward a world wide economic recession, food supplies grow shorter especially in third world countries, terrorism threatens us unabatedly, and local wars continue to flare up the world over. We all have psychological reasons for feeling victimized, and in this atmosphere of anxiety feeling grateful is not easily arrived at.

Recently, in the course of a synagogue conversation with my congregation on the subject of gratitude, when asked the reason for Jewish ingratitude and rage, one respondent pointed to the history of Jewish suffering. He understandably referred to the Holocaust as a natural and perfectly reasonable explanation for this background of resentment and ungratefulness that accompany this deeply embedded sense of victimization. "All I can feel is anger, anger at God for allowing this to happen," he said.

How could a people, living on the brink of disaster, enduring centuries of vulnerability, powerlessness, persecution and uncertainty, not articulate its fury and rage at God and at life in general, demanding some semblance of fairness and justice to sustain them?

A healthy Judaism need not be fixated on tragedy and persecution. It was Salo W. Baron, perhaps the greatest Jewish historian of this century, who devoted volumes of work to counteract a notion that had prevailed in Jewish historical thinking for much too long, namely the "lachrymose conception of Jewish history," an idea that suggested that the essence of Jewish reality is that of tragedy and tears. It was Baron's lifetime intention to alter that view and demonstrate that Jewish history is a proud and creative one, for which the Jewish people and the world should be grateful.[26]

My personal sense of victimization coincided, in an obviously grandiose way, with the understanding of Jewish experience as an amalgam of sufferings and defeats. The victim "Israel" and I shared a reality of being unjustly persecuted and deprived, creating a frame of mind that demanded victory and success by none other than God. After all, God had chosen Israel, and I had chosen God in order to feel like the chosen child. In this shadow of choseness, I too had every right to articulate my complaints and expect some reaffirmation of my special status by receiving rewards and special recognition.

As a young boy of 10 or 12, I found myself emotionally gravitating toward the Jewish experience of struggle and survival. I vividly recall my fascination with Jewish history dramatically expounded in 6th grade by a survivor of the Holocaust. The Holocaust seared a not uncommon question into my mind: Where was God during this unstoppable unfolding of inhumanity and cruelty? With the fury came psychological numbness, but also the emotional "benefits" of being the victim. One can derive a deep yet perverse sense of special ness, even superiority, through the perception of being chosen for suffering. The cry of—I am a Victim—must, by all moral standards of fairness and decency, find its way heavenwards and arouse the attention and favor of the ultimate Parent. My identity became connected to an unrelenting sense of victimization—"I am victim, therefore I am!" My deep-rooted identification with all things Jewish magnified my Jewish identity and sense of Jewish pride.

Victimization became a badge of honor. Paradoxically, the victim is often able to exercise great power over others. By gaining pity and concern via victimization, one acquires the protection and aid of the powerful. The "victim" or "underdog" is always in the right and is rarely held up to standards of responsibility by which the non-victim is judged.

The Bible defines the Israelite people as "'stiff-necked". This "cultural" characteristic could be seen as either a dogged determination to refuse to obey God's word, or it can point to a capacity of the Jew to pursue an unbending standard without compromise, accepting nothing less than the absolute ideal of one's expectation. While this deeply embedded inclination may have yielded the capacity to survive and much achievement over the centuries, it has likewise accounted for no small share of dissatisfaction and unhappiness, in addition to an almost unbendable inability to be grateful. Rage and victimization act not only as impediments to feeling grateful, however reasonable and justifiable, but also stand in the way of creating a relationship of trust and gratefulness with God. I believe that the alienation of many Jewish souls from the wellspring of gratefulness is tied intimately with their spiritual alienation from God and from the wisdom of Judaism.

The flip side of the fear of responsibility is the fear of losing God's protection. A curious and ironic roadblock to experiencing gratefulness among Jews and others who belong to monotheistic faith communities is linked to the understanding of the nature and function of God. Above all things, God is intimately concerned with the oppressed, the poor, and the disadvantaged, those who suffer and indeed complain. God hears the pleas of the underprivileged, the victim, and the powerless.

This response of faith fills the pages of the Bible and the prayer book. It is those in dire straits who seem to be most favored by God. If that is so, can we not conceive of an individual unconsciously preferring to remain among the unhappy and discontent so as to gain God's attention more readily and immediately? In a psychologically complex way, the persecutions and the sufferings of the Jewish people make it more natural and "comfortable" to feel deprived and dissatisfied as an act of attaining God's attention and concern. Like the child who attracts a parent's attention by behaving in a negative or a complaining manner, so too do we often find it easier to feel unfulfilled and unhappy as a means of managing our hoped-for response from God, a response of protection and love. To be happy, on the other hand, is to suggest according to this logic, that God will no longer be interested in our predicament because we have conveyed to God our ability to survive without God's providence. Happiness, in other words, could be understood psychologically as risking God's indifference, even abandonment, and a most terrifying psychological possibility.

Going Grateful

Write down or read the following poem when you awaken in the morning. It is a wonderful meditation; a spiritual introduction to the "Modeh Ani" prayer of Traditional Judaism recited each morning upon awakening.

Heart,
I implore you,
It's time to come back
From the dark,
It's morning,
The hills are pink
And the roses
whatever they felt
in the valley of night
are opening now
their soft dresses,
their leaves
are shining.
Why are you laggard?
Sure you have seen this
A thousand times,
Which isn't half enough.
Let the world
have its way with you,
Luminous as it is,
With mystery and pain-
Graced as it is
with the ordinary.[27]
　　　　　—Mary Oliver

A "gratefulness journal" can serve as an excellent way to enhance your awareness of the many things and people you may be grateful for. Since this journal will become a wellspring of feeling that will unlock the fullness of life, consider acquiring a special blank book that appeals to you in a particularly pleasing manner. Savor every aspect of this purchase; running your finger across the cover and pages, relishing any artistic beauty of its design, knowing that like a diary, this journal will become a cherished companion.

Each evening, consider at least three aspects in your day which elicit gratefulness. You may find an early morning hour more convenient for this practice. Record what you look forward to as reasons for being grateful on that particular day.

CHAPTER 3

FROM GREED TO GRATEFULNESS

The belief that we are entitled to satisfying all our desires can prevent us from being grateful for what we have or from recognizing the difference between what we want and need. Rabbi Harold Kushner says, "People who feel entitled . . . are never satisfied because they measure their wealth not by what they have but by what others have that they lack."[28] Envy of others is the opposite of gratitude. The only benefit in life for the envious person is that what he has gives him a competitive advantage; the only good is that which has a Me-up/you-down potential.

In an age of seductive advertising, which promises everything, feeling grateful is for some akin to settling for less. Preoccupation with a fantasy of what one deserves leads to an unwillingness or inability to accept anything less, contributing to an unyielding sense of incompleteness and unhappiness. Unless and until one gets everything, contentment remains unreachable—even undesirable. Once we have established a sense of entitlement, we are painfully vulnerable to the prospect of disappointment.

What are the sources of this sense of entitlement? Interestingly, they derive from two opposite poles on the psychological spectrum of our lives. On the one hand, if one is over-indulged, that is, catered to without restraint or limitation, never incorporating an ability to delay gratification, that person's sense of entitlement is without measure and rarely, if ever, can he be satisfied. Conversely, one who is persistently deprived may feel a gnawing sense of being entitled to anything and everything, as a way of being compensated for not receiving enough, and remains, likewise unfulfilled and ungrateful.

A common question that frequently arises is: If we are so rich, why aren't we happy? Research done on the subjective well being of people has shown that happiness cannot be bought. In the midst of our increasingly abundant culture, people don't seem to be getting any happier. The psychological reason for this phenomenon is the "law of habituation," which means that over time, we tend to get used to our current level of satisfaction, and then expect and demand even more of ourselves and of others. For example, a major league baseball player may not be happy (and perhaps may even feel deprived) with his $500,000 annual salary, because this has been his salary for the past five years, and other teammates are making much more."[29] This "law of habituation" contributes significantly to the fear one may have of missing out and being deprived.

The headline of a recent New York Times article, "The Millionaires Who Don't Feel Rich," sums it up well. The item described a community of working-class millionaires in Silicon Valley, California, accomplished and ambitious members of the digital elite (who) still do not think of themselves as particularly fortunate, in part because they are surrounded by people with more wealth-often a lot more. "You look around," Mr. Barbagallo said, "and the pressures to spend are everywhere. Children want the latest fashions their peers are wearing and the most popular high-ticket toys . . . . Spouses talk, and now that resort in Mexico the family enjoyed so much last winter is not good enough when looking ahead to next year" . . . To Mr. Milletti, it all looks like a marathon with no finish line. "Here the top 1 percent chases the top one-tenth of 1 percent, and the top one-tenth of 1 percent chases the top one-one-hundredth of 1 percent," he said.[30]

Two very different traditions arrive at the very same conclusion regarding the insatiability of human desire. In the book of Ecclesiastes (Koheleth), we are told: "He who loves money will never have enough of it—he who loves wealth will never attain it—this is indeed futility."[31] Buddhism's Sacred Writings, the Dhammapada, likewise declare that the craving for things is a source of spiritual harm: "Wealth harms the greedy but not those who seek nirvana; of little understanding the greedy harm themselves and those around them . . . Selfish desire ruins the mind as weeds ruin the fields."[32]

Our rabbis inform us: "Who is rich? He who is content with his portion."[33] By recognizing the myriad gifts embodied in life and not looking elsewhere with greed and envy we can consider ourselves as rich in spirit and in genuine self-regard. Each one of us is given a piece, a portion of life, as a remarkable gift. The challenge is to be grateful for that portion which is unique to each one of us.

Going Grateful

List one thing in your life for which you are grateful. Record it in your journal or scrapbook. Try to describe it in greater detail; consider all the contours of what you are grateful for and why it is so important to you. The item need not be a complicated or abstract one; a simple, everyday thing could arouse many associations of feeling of gratitude. For example, the object of consideration could be the delicious cereal you had for breakfast, an ordinary yet favorite easy chair, and a familiar scent you enjoy at the moment.

If you prefer an activity that does not require writing or recording, sit quietly and comfortably, close your eyes and think about your one gift. Allow the feelings and thoughts to surface as they relate to this object of gratitude. If your mind wanders, gently return to the subject of your gratitude and make room in your mind and heart for its consideration. A few minutes of this practice could be a source of calm and joy in your day.

In his book Stopping, David Kudntz suggests the practice of "Stillpoints." When waiting in line, driving the car, riding a bus or subway, during brief intervals between tasks, stop for a moment and consider the good things for which you can be grateful-these stillpoints will change your life.

CHAPTER 4

FROM GUILT TO GRATEFULNESS

Gratitude is the moral memory of mankind—Georg Simmel

We often attack ourselves with self-recrimination and guilt, convincing ourselves that we are in fact undeserving and unworthy of any gifts, joy, success or beneficence from the world or from God. Consequently, we are left incapable of being thankful—for anything. If I don't get what I really want, we say, perhaps it's because I am not good enough. We are left with a feeling of persistent self-denigration and inferiority.

The psychological culprit of inappropriate undeservedness is often a lurking sense of guilt that spreads through the psyche and persuades us that "Because I have *done* something bad, I *am* bad." But, there is a world of difference between "wrong-doing" and "wrong-being."

The rabbis of the Talmud recognized this important distinction in the following story:

> "There were once some highwaymen in the neighborhood of Rabbi Meir who caused him much trouble. He accordingly prayed that they should die. His wife Beruriah said to him: 'How can you recite such a prayer? It is written—"Let sins cease." (Psalms104: 35) Is it written sinners? Since it is further written, "let the sinners be no more," does not this prove that once the sins (the behavior) ceases likewise there will no longer be any evil men! Rather pray for them that they should repent.' He did, and they repented."[34]

Sinners cannot be grateful; humans, who sin, can. To deem oneself as a sinner, namely as one inherently predisposed to sin, one whose identity is a dark and evil one, is to place overwhelming obstacles in the way of human improvement and spiritual attainment. The burden of one who sees himself as bad is so great that the awareness of the grateful is beyond one's grasp. While the perspective of gratefulness does not ignore the capacity of the human to do the wrong and the sinful, it holds out the promise of change and betterment rather than dwelling on the alleged innate sinfulness of the person.

No one enjoys feeling guilty. I am acquainted with many clergypersons who use guilt as a powerful tool of persuasion. It does bring about some changed behavior and desired responses of greater commitment to religious life, but I believe that this success is short-lived and comes with a high emotional price. Change is not only brief, but when of longer duration it is accompanied by an underlying resentment and a feeling of being imposed upon, being obligated without a sense of personal desire and positive acceptance. Guilt makes people angry, often contributing to a negative frame of mind, which exhibits itself in unnecessary responses of recrimination toward others and oneself.

The psycho-religious experience of guilt and self-blame, so pervasive in Western religious thought and behavior, should, I believe, be replaced by the cultivation of the inborn capacity to live, feel, and act on the basis of gratefulness. Instead of guilt, why not gratefulness as an impetus and psychological motivation for right and moral behavior?

Many argue that guilt is necessary if we are to maintain a moral society and a moral life. One who does not feel guilt presents us with the terrible risk of anti-social behavior that can have devastating results. Indeed, at times it is both healthy and necessary to feel guilt. Not to sense responsibility for a wrongdoing is a sign of emotional immaturity and callousness.

Yet, I have become more and more convinced that guilt arising out of fear of punishment is less and less an effective moral instrument for the realization of goodness and justice in our society. Guilt lessens and damages the integrity and wholeness of the ego, while gratefulness nurtures and endows it with a greater capacity to live compassionately and caringly. Human relationships, especially the more intimate ones that affect members of a family, when influenced by guilt, create an exacerbation of negative and painful experiences, often contributing to a family environment of tension and the desire to either hurt or escape. The parent who conveys an honest sense of gratefulness for her children, with all their shortcomings and failures, has a much greater likelihood of successful child rearing than a caregiver who persists in punishing and inflicting guilt as an "educational" tool.

Guilt is grounded in narcissism. Guilt suggests," *I* feel bad." When one is guilt-ridden and decides to change his behavior, often the motivation is to remove the feelings of discomfort that one feels; it is a selfish response. In contrast, when one feels grateful for life and for others, the need to change or improve is centered on the feeling and awareness that the other person feels badly as a result of one's misbehavior or wrongdoing. Thus, this feeling is outer-directed and very much connected to the sensitivities of another human being, reflecting a sense of greater altruism, emotional maturity, and social responsibility.

If we feel undeserving of happiness and therefore feel persistently ungrateful, would not the shift away from guilt enhance a more positive feeling about ourselves, allowing us to feel better about who we are and to thus discover the inner resource of gratefulness? In other words, guilt can be a serious hurdle on the path toward gratefulness and should be removed to clear the way to greater self-realization that comes with the fundamental awareness of the gift of life in all its myriad manifestations.

When one experiences gratefulness for a particular gift—life, nature, loved ones, health or material possessions—one is strongly motivated to care for and cherish those gifts. Admonitions and threats of punishment or pain fall considerably short as moral rationales for furthering proper, positive and life-enhancing behavior. Greater awareness of the giftedness of what we are and what we have, generating a sense of gratefulness, engenders a response of concern and respect for one another and for our world.

One of the major preoccupations of contemporary life is the well-being and care of our natural environment. This attention is dominating our lives, from young to old, from the highest level politician to the average person on the street, with no regard to race, gender, religion or creed. Its arching embrace is obvious; this is our only home and we need to take care of it and sustain it. The ways by which we are educated to higher environmental consciousness are myriad. From kindergarten class trips to the nearby park to science projects conducted in high school laboratories, the wonders of nature and its fragility, the interconnectedness of all things and the need to take responsibility for our planetary home, are all compressed into the grateful awareness of all of life as a gift. This is an axis of natural intersection between science and religion. The teaching of wonder transcends ideology and belief. It is a universal perspective shared by all. To teach respect for nature from the vantage point of guilt is short lived and negative, creating a climate of fear rather than one of wondrous gratitude and love. To protect the environment from guilt generates a sense of resentment toward the world rather than an attitude of care and authentic respect. As in the total spiritual approach to life, gratefulness grooms the soul for compassion and concern while guilt grinds the human spirit into the dust of discontent and dread.

Perhaps the cultivation of gratefulness that carries with it a renewed sense of the importance of all aspects of life as expressions of gifts bestowed upon us, will remind us and future generations that sustaining life is based on our gratefulness for it.

In his discussion on the meaning of praise during the celebration of Passover, Rabbi Joseph B. Soloveitchick, perhaps the most outstanding Orthodox thinker of our time, understands the natural and organic connection between praise, i.e. gratefulness, and ethical conduct. When one celebrates the Passover holiday the liturgy reminds us that the purpose of Passover is to "'Remember the exodus from Egypt." This act of remembering is a spiritual invitation to elicit a deep sense of gratitude for the liberation from slavery and link that inner perception to an external act of compassion and goodness. In other words, memory is summoned in the service of ethical behavior. "Why are we permitted to say "shir va-shevah"—songs of praise—to God? True, we cannot help ourselves. But there is another answer. To praise God means that whatever we say of God becomes a guiding principle for our actions. Whatever God does to us, we are supposed to do to others. Since God feeds us, we must feed the hungry and the destitute. Since God is "malbish arumim," since He clothes people, we must buy clothes for those who walk around in rags . . . . Since God visits the sick, we are called upon to do likewise. Every praise, every attribute that we ascribe to God turns into moral law, an ethical principle."[35]

The prayer—"I am grateful in Your Presence"—holds out a psychological reality not based on the approval or accolades of others, but rather the awareness of "lefanecha"—"before You." I am alive because I am in Your Presence. You are the gracious and generous Giver. Consequently, the "I", one's sense of who one is, is derived essentially from the recognition of receiving an immeasurable gift, of deserving life in all its myriad manifestations and being thankful.

Closely connected with feelings of not deserving is the fear of being happy. This sounds like the most unlikely and illogical of all obstacles to gratefulness, yet it is quite pervasive and real. Many of us are terrified of happiness and often feel guilt when we experience happiness. Again and again I experience the feeling myself and meet people who share the same fear. Something good happens, I feel content and grateful. Then lo and behold, my mind becomes cluttered with unstoppable thoughts of impending doom and disaster. Before you know it, the joy of the positive has degenerated into anxiety and fear.

Not long ago I shared with a colleague my good fortune at having found a new apartment in an area where my wife and I had been looking for only a short time. The cost was reasonable, the space was more than adequate, and the sellers were lovely people whom we trusted—we felt grateful and fortunate. As I enthusiastically described our apartment hunting with its happy ending, I was suddenly overcome with a feeling that something would happen to interfere with the realization of this wonderful stroke of good luck. I was not going to get the prize. Curiously, whenever the telephone rang or the mail arrived I was convinced that the call or piece of mail would inform me that the apartment had been sold to someone else. I didn't deserve it! I was destined not to have it! It was too good to be true! Quickly and instantaneously, I would, as my psychoanalyst many years before would repeatedly point out, "Snatch defeat out of the jaws of victory."

"That's exactly what my mother would say," a friend once said. "Why do we do this?" she asked. "I don't understand why it is so difficult to be happy, to hold on to the feeling of being happy, as if it is safer to be sad!"

We are terrified of joy; something deep within our psyches holds up a sign that reads: Thou shalt not be happy! Is it any wonder that we struggle so to arrive at the point of gratitude and thankfulness that lies in wait for our attention and acknowledgement?

Years ago, as a practicing social worker, I was treating the young adult son of a Holocaust survivor. His problem was his inability to feel angry with his parents, especially his father who was inclined to emotionally abuse him by being harshly critical. The roadblock to his rage was his anticipation of bottomless guilt at the prospect of causing pain to a victim of the Holocaust who had endured the utmost conceivable level of human suffering and pain. The slightest emotional hint of getting angry was simply unbearable. Consequently, he was entrapped in an emotional world empty of any happiness or personal pleasure. Gratefulness was beyond his reach. To feel happy was psychologically interpreted as an act of betrayal of his parent's brutal experience. How could he be happy when his parents suffered so? To perpetuate his loyalty and attachment to his surviving parents he was emotionally obligated to share their pain and in this way perpetuate a state of unhappiness. To deviate from this pattern suggested an abandonment of his parents in a deeply emotional way.

Who hasn't felt at one time or another, when enjoying something or feeling particularly happy, that others, if they knew of our good fortune, would become angry and envious, resulting in a loss of social acceptance and perhaps even subjecting you to some danger stemming from this jealousy. Subconsciously, the prospect of a hex or curse makes gratefulness too risky an emotion to experience! Is this not in part a reason for the popular Jewish folk superstition of the *ayin ha'ra*, the "evil eye?" Commonly, whenever something good is hoped for or expected, it is accompanied by the utterance of "*k 'nayn ein horah*"-lit.without the evil eye!

To cultivate feelings of gratefulness in ourselves and help others feel grateful, not guilty, in our efforts to bring about the necessary changes in our lives, is both a challenge and a delight. It is not guilt but gratefulness that will lead to a world of greater goodness and well-being.

Going Grateful

PRAISED ARE YOU THE SOURCE OF FORGIVENESS.

Whether in the western world where guilt is prevalent or the culture of the East dominated by feelings of shame when wrongdoing is committed, we all share a sense of moral ineptitude. Our mortality is a constant reminder of our moral imperfection. We feel trapped in our feeling bad, unworthy, inadequate even sinful. We wish to escape the pain of self-reproach.

Focus on forgiveness. Let go of the burden of guilt; forgive your failures and those of others, recognize your inner goodness, and that of others

> I THANK YOU FOR THE GIFT OF FORGIVENESS
> I THANK YOU FOR FORGIVING ME.
> I THANK YOU FOR THE ABILITY TO FORGIVE MYSELF
> I AM GRATEFUL TO BE ABLE TO FORGIVE OTHERS.

In your "Gratefulness journal" describe an event or situation that made you feel guilty. Write a detailed description, focusing on your feelings when the incident occurred and how you feel now. Consider something related to the experience that you could feel grateful about and record it in your journal.

CHAPTER 5

FROM GRANDIOSITY TO GRATEFULNESS

"I am perfect, therefore I am!" For many people, a compulsive need for independence can be a deeply debilitating emotional and spiritual liability.

Rabbi Harold Kushner, in his recent book "The Lord is My Shepherd," answers the question of why gratefulness is so elusive in this way: "There are people who . . . need to feel self-sufficient . . . the receiving end of the gift might make us feel weak and needy."[36] We resist admitting our vulnerability and our natural and necessary dependence on others. We don't like to feel obligated or indebted to anyone else, and in some minds the notion of feeling grateful arouses feelings of owing something, a psychological onus that robs an individual of her sense of independence and individuality. We do everything we can to control our lives and not feel vulnerable to outside forces. So much of our life's energy is dedicated to enhancing and protecting our power, our sense of mastery over our lives that the slightest intimation of being grateful and receptive is terrifying.

In fact, we are all dependent on others; to be human is to be dependent. But sensing this dependency can be frightening, and so we try desperately to avoid or ignore it. The sense that we owe something to someone—a friend, a spouse, a child or God—imposes a heavy psychological burden that exposes our false sense of self-sufficiency, leaving us feeling that we cannot live freely and completely.

The American ethos emphasizing independence as the loftiest goal interferes with the spiritual possibility that we can derive from recognizing our dependence on others and the consequent feeling of gratefulness that flows from this recognition. Studies conducted about a decade ago by an Israeli sociologist, Shula Sommers, concluded that American men, in general, found gratitude to be a "humiliating emotion-"[37] probably because it implied dependence on others.

Prior to the summer Olympic games of 2004, PBS television ran an illuminating program on the games' history and significance. Reputable professors were on hand to lend knowledge and insight to this subject.

In ancient Greece we were told, the games were perhaps the most important of all religious events. They represented the ideal of emulating, if not surpassing, the gods in achieving perfection of the human body and mind and exceeding mortal limits of physical strength and endurance. Zeus, the head of the pagan pantheon of gods, symbolized that idea. The highest objective of the ancient athlete was to gain victory. To go out in a blaze of glory, even to lose one's life in the course of winning, was regarded as the apogee of human accomplishment.

But Daniel Mendelsohn, a lecturer in the classics at Princeton University saw it differently. About its ideology and ethos, he said: "The ancient Greeks' way of thinking has more in common with the relentless egotism, nationalism, promotion and self-promotion we associate with current professional sports than with any fantasy of the noble Greek spirit." [38]

He also pointed out that several of the key features of contemporary Olympics originated not with the ancient Greeks but rather with the 1936 Olympic games held in Nazi Germany. To glorify the perfection and superiority of the Aryan race, the Nazi government deliberately introduced the carrying of the torch, the rings on the Olympic flag, and the nature of the Olympics as a grand spectacle. In other words, the obsession with perfection was inextricably linked to an ideological "perfectionism" that led to the most heinous crime ever witnessed by humanity.

I have no intention of demeaning the achievements, excitement and ideals of the Olympics as a demonstration of peaceful cooperation and competition among nations. I am convinced, however, that much of the underlying passion for the Olympic enterprise, the obsession with and adoration of perfectionism, can be, and is, a contemporary affliction of the human spirit. The dividing line between a sense of natural self-respect, even pride, and that of arrogance and grandiosity is a thin one. The need to win, to defeat the opponent as an expression of one's superiority and perfection often outstrips the opportunity of engaging in international competition as a demonstration of sportsmanship and collaboration. Anything short of a gold medal assumes not an attitude of gratitude but a response of disappointment and resentment.

The importance of the esthetic, the health of the human body, and the desirability of ambition and pursuing excellence in all worthy undertakings are entirely legitimate and desirable. An Orthodox Jewish spokesman of the stature of Rabbi Joseph B. Soloveitchik reminds us that: "Man reaching for the distant stars is acting in harmony with his nature which was created, willed and directed by his Maker." [39]

However, the loftiest human goal is not a blaze of glory but a blessing of gratefulness, the flicker of faith, the holiness of hope and harmony.

Unlike the Greek ideal of breaking the mold of mortality and transcending death by achieving immortality through feats of perfection, the spiritual approach to life acknowledges mortality and imperfection and sees as its ideal not the surpassing of the material and mortal but their sanctification. Earthliness cannot be eradicated or escaped, but it can be the arena in which and from which the divine can be extracted and elevated; the physical is the raw material out of which a life of spiritual artistry can be fashioned. Like an artist who perceives the world from the point of view of the internal, universal and meaningful, even the divine, religion's purpose is to transform the reality of this world into moments of spiritual beauty, goodness and compassion.

The notion of imitatio *dei*, emulating God, never for a moment intimates the remotest possibility of being comparable to or surpassing God. To consider this prospect would be the most egregious act of hubris, utter folly and perilous to one's life-"No man may see me and live"[40] we are told in the book of Exodus.

Startling as it may seem, the Bible and rabbinic literature suggest that God Himself is not perfect. The references that indicate the vulnerability of God are often explained by turning to an established dictum of rabbinic literature that "the Torah expresses itself in the language that is comprehensible to humans," thus the use of descriptions that anthropomorphize God. For example, the Torah recounts how God was disappointed with the behavior of humans and "the Lord regretted that He had made man on earth."[41] Throughout the Bible God is pictured as experiencing a wide range of human emotions. Does this suggest the limitation of language when it comes to explaining God? Perhaps. Yet I am convinced that when we are told of God's regret, somehow God's "imperfection" is reflected. God first experiment in creating a "perfect" world failed, leaving Him no choice but to start again. A fascinating Talmudic interpretation goes even further disclosing not only God's imperfection but also God's need for forgiveness and atonement from humans.

"Rabbi Shimon ben Pazi posed the following contradiction: It is written-'And God created the two great luminaries,' and written immediately after it is written- ' . . . the greater luminary to dominate the day and the lesser luminary to dominate the night.' The first phrase signifies equality between the sun and moon and the second tells us that the moon is not as great as the sun. How do we reconcile these statements?

The moon said before the Holy One Blessed Be He, 'Master of the Universe? Is it possible for two kings to utilize the same crown?' God said to her: 'Go and diminish yourself.' The moon then said before God: 'Master of the Universe—Is it fitting that because I said the correct thing before You I must diminish myself?' . . . He said to her: 'Go and let Israel reckon the days and years through you.' She said to Him: 'But the sun also serves in this capacity?' . . . The moon was not mollified, therefore the Holy One, Blessed is He, said to His people: 'Bring an atonement on my behalf for having diminished the moon.'

And this is the meaning of that which Rabbi Shimon Ben Lakish has said: 'Why is the he-goat of the New Month (which is determined by the position of the moon) different from other he-goats brought on other festive occasions, for the phrase-'for God'—is stated regarding the New Month? (This phrase is absent in the descriptions of the sacrifices brought on other occasions.) The Holy One replied: 'This he-goat shall be an atonement for My having diminished the moon.'"

This rabbinic excerpt conveys the radical thought that God needs the human to atone for him, suggesting God's "imperfectability." Flowing from this conclusion is the recognition and acceptance of the imperfections of the human being. Since humans were created in God's image, it follows that this image refracts that which is imperfect. Thus the onerous burden of perfection is removed not only from the "shoulders" of the Almighty, but from those of humans as well.

The pursuit of perfection can be viewed as justifiable, even beneficial. However, when this insatiable appetite for perfection overreaches itself and ignores the need to recognize human limitation and frailty, the obsession is not only unhealthy psychologically but spiritually hazardous as well.

Abraham Joshua Heschel stated this principle dramatically and succinctly when he pointed out that: "We are never told "Hear O Israel, the Lord our God the Lord is Perfect!" It is an attribute that is strikingly absent in both biblical and rabbinic literature."[42] Rather we recite twice daily: "Hear O Israel, the Lord our God the Lord is One." To strive for unity, harmony and peace is to do God's bidding.

In the wise words of Sarah Ban Breathnach: "A point worth pondering: Upon completing the Universe, the great Creator pronounced it "Very good." Not "Perfect.""

It takes great inner strength to tolerate imperfection in oneself. Perhaps the obsession with perfection today is a "reaction formation" to the confusion and fear that seem to surround us at this time. We are being seduced into thinking that there is only one truth or one way to happiness and a growing fundamentalism in all faith communities is becoming a dangerous reality of contemporary life.

To me there are many streams of thought and belief, all of which emerge from, and return to, the oceanic vastness and endlessness of what I refer to as God. The spirit of sincere pluralism and respect for diversity can offer much needed perspective and clarity to the confusion and challenges of today.

We live in a culture of confusion. No one approach to any problem is definitive or comprehensive. Psychiatry may help, but biological and genetic factors have to be taken into consideration, one's temperament is significant, the culture around us and our basic existential condition of living is something we have to live with and accept.

In a Path With Heart by Jack Kornfield, one of the qualities of spiritual maturity is described as non-idealism by which "the heart can turn the suffering and imperfections we encounter into a path of compassion . . . . Mature spirituality is not based on seeking perfection . . . . it is based on the capacity to let go and to love, to open the heart to all that is . . . . in this non-idealistic practice, the divine can shine through even in acts of ignorance and fear, inviting us to wonder at the mystery of all that is."[43]

Rachel Naomi Remen, in *Kitchen Table Wisdom*, expresses her understanding of perfectionism's peril this way: "The pursuit of perfection has become the addiction of our time! Children can learn early that they are loved for what they do and not simply for who they are . . . the life of such children can become a constant striving to earn love. Of course, love is never earned. It is a grace we give one another. Anything we need to earn is only approval . . . . Perfectionism is so widespread in this culture that we actually had to invent another word for love. 'Unconditional love,' we say. Yet, all love is unconditional. Anything else is just approval."[44]

With the spiritual perception of gratefulness, we have an opportunity to deal with our lives in such a way that our material success, fame and fortune, will become secondary to the inner life that we experience deeply, our moral sense of what is right and wrong, and the meaning and purpose of our lives. I am quite persuaded that in the realm of the human spirit, humility and integrity that come with gratefulness, not grandiosity, are the greatest of all human rewards.

In addressing audiences regarding the spiritual imperative of gratefulness, one concern that reappears repeatedly is framed in the following question: "If we are grateful, what will happen to ambition, to the desire to advance? Won't this lead to passivity and resignation?" To the contrary. Gratefulness is not synonymous with self-satisfaction or complacency. If one were cynical about life, fatalistic, then perhaps the eventual outcome would be one of indifference and inaction. Likewise, if one felt entirely entitled, this sense of entitlement would bring about a consequence of sitting back and awaiting the showering of gifts from above, without the need for any human exertion or effort.

When one is imbued with gratefulness, one considers all of life from a perspective of life's preciousness and fragility which demands careful attention and sacred stewardship, a response of on-going investment and effort to preserve and to better the gifts for which we are so profoundly and unceasingly grateful. Gratefulness engenders ambition for the well being of all. In other words, as will later be explained in the context of Jewish living, gratefulness sows the seeds of generosity and compassion, tangible translations into action of thoughts and feelings intimately tied to an awareness of the "giftedness" of human existence.

Going Grateful:

As you take care of your morning hygienic and grooming activities, looking into the mirror, notice the beauty in your face, the color of your eyes, the contours of your cheeks, and the shape of your nose. While you may find yourself engaging in some self-criticism, unhappy with the way you look, consider the wonder of every part of your face and with gratefulness for the gift of your face, recognize its unique beauty, knowing that your face is singular, that only you possess it.

Recite silently:

BLESSED ARE YOU WHO HAS MADE ME IN THE DIVINE IMAGE.

Again, in your gratefulness journal or sitting quietly for a few minutes, list or think about five things that you consider to be ideal or "perfect" about you for which you are grateful.

Conversely, do the same exercise but this time think of or list five things that you feel are not perfect in your life yet you are grateful for them.

Bring to mind a loved one or friend and list five things about them that are perfect for which you are grateful or five things about them that fall short of the 'ideal' yet you can feel grateful for them.

CHAPTER 6

FROM GRIEF TO GRATEFULNESS

"The highest tribute to the dead is not grief but gratitude"
—Thornton Wilder.

THE KADDISH-Sanctification

Magnified and sanctified be God's great name
In this world, created as God willed.
May God's sovereignty be established
In your lifetime
And the life of the entire House of Israel
Speedily and soon:
And let us say: Amen
May God's great Name be blessed forever,
In all worlds, unto eternity
Blessed, praised and glorified,
Extolled and honored,
Adorned, exalted and acclaimed
Be the name of the Holy One
Beyond all prayer and song,
Praise and consolation
That may be uttered in this world;
And let us say: Amen
May there be abundant divine peace.
Bringing good life to us,
And for all Israel:

And let us say: Amen
May the One who creates heavenly peace
Create peace for us and for all Israel:
And let us say: Amen.

The Kaddish is a prayer interspersed throughout each worship service as a marker of division between one segment and another. It is recognized in popular culture as the Jewish prayer for mourners but it is in reality simply one of the prayers said at several points during the service. What is notable is that the Kaddish said by mourners says nothing about grief or death, but just praises God.

As an expression of praise, the Kaddish is a formal articulation of a sense of gratefulness to God. What makes the Kaddish such an extraordinary liturgical expression of gratefulness is that it is recited at the time of greatest grief and sadness, the time of death. We seem to be confronted with a blatant contradiction. To thank God so effusively when a loved one dies seems to be the highest form of insensitivity, even emotional cruelty. How then can we make spiritual sense of a prayer that praises God in the face of the very antithesis of life?

It is precisely at this time that we understand the wisdom of Jewish liturgy. The Kaddish summons the sufferer to stretch his or her spiritual and emotional resources in order to touch a spot of gratefulness deep within the soul, to catch an emotional glimpse of a reality beyond the immediacy of pain and loss, to see a vastness and endlessness that gives hope and the ability to move forward and transform death into a moment of deeper wisdom and love. The Kaddish helps us journey from "Nothingness" to "Eternity."

The phrase—"leaylah min kol birchata"—"beyond all praise and song"—instructs us that when we utter praise we reach for a level of reality that transcends death and time. This is the precise juncture in our lives when more than ever we are in need of a sense of spaciousness and peacefulness in which we may feel embraced and cared for by a God who is ultimately the Giver and Provider of all things.

The Kaddish propels us to a place beyond a reality that we know and have experienced. "Leayla min kol birchata"-above and beyond all blessings, above and beyond all reasons to praise. All of life is reason to praise, to be grateful. Gratefulness, however, halts at the gates of death. Where is the God of Gratefulness, the Giver of all things when all we face is disruption, destruction and emptiness? At death we meet mystery, the realm of the non-rational, that aspect of the divine that "takes back," that "takes away," that adumbrates with infinite "nothingness." We seemed to have reached the end of the line. We have arrived at a point in our experience that transcends the necessity, desirability or appropriateness of gratefulness and praise.

"Beyond all praise!" Where is God at this time? In the words of Rabbi Joseph Soloveitchik, "ecstatic adoration, even expressed in hymn, is not prayer. The latter transcends the bounds of liturgical worship and must not be reduced to its external-technical aspects such as praise, thanksgiving or even petition. Prayer is basically an awareness of man finding himself in the presence of and addressing himself to his Maker, and to pray has one connotation only: To stand before God . . . the very essence of prayer is the covenantal experience of being together with and talking to God . . . Prayer is the continuation of prophecy . . ."[45]

At the point of death, the Kaddish tells us that in the midst of our shattered selves we can enter into a unique relationship with God that takes us beyond the relationships of giver and recipient, of past gratefulness. Out of the anguish of death, lonely man encounters lonely God. "Shema Yisrael"—"Hear O Israel, the Lord is our God, the Lord is One." This core declaration of Jewish faith strikingly brings home the realization of unique man converging with the incomparable Oneness of God and simply being in God's presence becomes the ultimate spiritual ideal.

But, at death we also encounter the angelic arena, praying for a peace that can only originate in heaven-"shalom bemromav", peace on High. After all is said and done, there is no other reality but the angelic aspiration to praise.

Soloveitchik continues: "This prayer is a praise of God, an awareness that, far from being insignificant like the beasts of the field, man is important enough for God Himself to be concerned with his praise. Saying Kaddish, then, is a defiance of death, a statement not only about the greatness of God, but about the greatness of man."[46]

How fitting and spiritually uplifting it is that we are reminded of our "angelic" capacity to praise God when our mortality as human beings menacingly stares us in the face with its terror and its pain. In doing so, therefore, we elevate our lives from the depths of despair and grief to the heights of faith and renewal. Gratefulness becomes a path leading toward human greatness.

In the Jewish mystical tradition, the human is endowed with the spiritual capacity to influence the very nature and identity of God. In a commentary on the Kaddish, a great rabbi of the 18th century, Rabbi Jacob Emden, points out that there are ten expressions of praise in the Kaddish that correspond to the ten "sefirot," the ten manifestations of God's Presence, suggesting that

God needs our praise so as to regain His full greatness and holiness. [47] A similar concept is articulated by the Pulitzer prize winner in literature, S.Y. Agnon: "When one of the house of Israel dies, there is a loss of glory in His kingdom, and His grandeur is diminished . . . let us pray for ourselves and for Him too that He and His kingdom be hallowed and enhanced, glorified and celebrated."[48]

The rabbis tell us: "In the same way that one is required to recite a blessing praising God for the good, like wise are we obligated to pronounce a blessing for the bad."[49] Again it appears as if the tradition is unfeeling and unfair. But in fact, as we recite the blessing we are called upon to consider all the gifts in the life of the deceased and all the blessing yet to be enjoyed. In other words, as we bless we say thank you to God for his being our Giver of all things.

The Rabbis recognized the almost impossible task for the human heart to bless when experiencing being "cursed." Yet, they held out the challenge and possibility of transcending the hurt and desire to retaliate emotionally with cursing rather than blessing, and emphasized the unique spiritual capacity of the human being to rise above such natural feelings and find a way to praise in the face of adversity and nothingness. Rabbi Akiva valiantly declares: "Everything that God does He does for the good!"[50]

> "I am not ready to die,
> But I am learning to trust death
> As I have trusted life.
> I am moving
> Toward a new freedom
> Born of detachment,
> And a sweeter grace-
> Learning to let go.
> I am not ready to die,
> But as I approach sixty,
> I turn my face toward the sea.
> I shall go where tides replace time,
> Where my world will open to a far horizon
> Over the floating, never-still flux and change.
> I shall go with the changes,
> I shall look far out over golden grasses
> And blue waters
> There are no farewells

> *Praise God for His mercies,*
> *For His austere demands,*
> *For His light,*
> *And for His darkness"*[51]
> —Mary Sarton

An integral part of the traditional funeral liturgy is the public pronouncement of the passage from Job 1:21, which reflects an understanding of death within the context of a give-and-take life process. "The Lord has given and the Lord has taken; praised be the name of the Lord!" God is praised for the totality of life, which inescapably and inevitably encompasses dynamics of giving and taking, gaining and losing.

This process is a natural one and one that we all experience in the course of our lives. In the insightful words of Brother Steidl-Rost: "Mere giving is as lifeless as mere taking. If you merely take a breath and stop there, you are dead. And when you merely breathe out and stop there, you are also dead. Life is not giving or taking but give-and-take . . . . it is the dynamic expression of universal belonging."[52] If one understands life as merely an experience of taking and is grateful only under circumstances of receiving, then his or her spiritual view of life is skewed, if not stunted. The rhythm of life is such that the breathing process requires both the taking in of air, inhaling, and the letting out, the giving away of air, exhaling. In like manner, our bodies discover balance as we ingest food and then expel it. The very physiology and biology of life are the bases and foundation for the spiritual principle of life's inevitable dynamic of giving and taking.

Interestingly, the book of Job ends with the full recognition by Job of the "allness" and inclusive wonder and vastness of life which then leads him to a final understanding of his position in the world as he declares: "Behold, my eyes have seen You, have witnessed Your reality."[53]

When the great poet and humanist Czeslaw Milosz died at the age of 93, Leon Weiselter, the distinguished literary editor of The New Republic, paid a stunning tribute to Milosz and concluded his words this way: "And then I thought that my friend, in his richness and his resilience, had truly been granted all the destinies. He had come to work and to laugh and to live and to die. And so mourning is now restrained by thanksgiving, as blessed Milosz would have wished."

"You gave me gifts, God-Enchanter
I gave you thanks for good and ill.
Eternal light in everything on earth.
As now, so on the day after my death."[54]

Going Grateful

There is a Jewish tradition that at the end of the seven-day mourning period, the Shiva, mourners walk around the block to signify their return to a normal pace of life.

This walk could be used as a way by which to heighten our gratefulness for our ability to walk both physically and emotionally, especially in the midst of grief and sorrow. The walking meditation can be a practice that is meaningful anytime.

We may consider the gift of mobility and recite:

BLESSED ARE YOU WHO GUIDES THE STEPS OF ALL LIVING CREATURES.
I AM GRATEFUL FOR EACH STEP THAT I AM ABLE TO TAKE.

Be mindful of each step, the miracle of being able to stand and move one leg ahead of the other. We do not have to walk in space or on water to recognize the wonder of walking. Walking on the solid earth is wonder enough. If not able to walk, look out a window at the sky, the trees, people walking by, the unending flow of life.

Look carefully around you.

Notice the objects: Their textures, their lines, their shapes, and their colors.

If your mind wanders, focus on one object and stay with it until its unique quality appears.

Name what you see.
Flower blooming
Rock resting
Sky shimmering
Street stretching
All is a gift-I am grateful.

For the mourner, an exercise in gratefulness could be helpful and therapeutic. Write down in your gratitude journal the qualities in the departed person for which you are grateful. Try to recall experiences and memories with the deceased that brought you a special sense of joy, those things that you miss the most.

Review the period of Shiva, the funeral, and the visitations and consider the people and their help at this difficult time for which you are grateful.

Take out photographs of loved ones or family pictures from childhood and include them in your "gratefulness scrapbook." Viewing videos or listening to the voices of loved ones on audio recordings can bring grateful comfort to mourners at this time.

PART TWO

There is only wonder, the realization that the world is too incredible, too meaningful for us. The existence of the world is the most unlikely, the most unbelievable fact. Even our ability for surprise is beyond expectation.[55]

Abraham Joshua Heschel

CHAPTER 7

Existence as Gratefulness: *"I Am therefore I Thank"*

On an existential level, the consideration of gratefulness may suggest, in some deeply felt way, a surrendering to the inevitability of mortality and finitude. Ernest Becker, in his classic work "The Denial of Death," quotes a well-known psychoanalyst Gregory Zilboorg as saying: "No one is free of the fear of death . . . . The anxiety neuroses, the various phobic states, even a considerable number of depressive suicidal states and many schizophrenias amply demonstrate the ever-present fear of death . . . we may take for granted that the fear of death is always present in our mental functioning."[56]

As long as one harbors a feeling of limitations it is possible to perpetuate the illusion that mortality can be denied, at least deferred. The more one moves in the direction of wanting more and engaging in an "expansive organismic striving"[37], the greater the sense of repression that is fostered as a defense against the reality of one's eventual mortality. Ernest Becker points out that "On the most elemental level the organism works actively against its own fragility by seeking to expand and perpetuate itself in living experience; instead of shrinking, it moves toward more life."[57] Desire is a deterrent against death. As Henri Bergson puts it: "Every human action has its starting point in a dissatisfaction, and thereby in a feeling of absence."[58] Interestingly inactivity, paralysis, even death, can be experienced as the possible result of surrendering the restless dissatisfaction that many feel. Thus, the feeling of gratefulness-not feeling dissatisfied—could suggest acquiescence to death.

As we mature we lose sight of the importance of the here and now and find ourselves shifting attention to the past and the future. Unlike the child who is totally immersed in the now, exhibiting an unvarnished sense of wonder and enchantment about everything, from the wave of water on the seashore to the twinkling of the distant star, grown-ups by contrast slip into thinking patterns preoccupied with the "what if" of both the past and the future. We review the past with a critical and recriminating attitude, trying to rewrite the dusty pages of ancient scripts. Others retreat to yesterday to take refuge in the nostalgia of days gone by, all the while ignoring and neglecting the gift of unfolding time in the present.

Moreover, often we encounter the community of planners, those whose fullest involvement is with the future. I knew of someone whose entire life was devoted to so-called "five-year plans." She would set out for herself a list of projected goals to be accomplished over five years; when that period passed it was time for another "five-year plan". Her mind was dominated by the extent to which she accomplished her designated goals, the ability of living in the moment significantly diminished.

The obsessive goal-oriented person lives in and for the future, unable to reap the joy and blessing of the now that transpires before him. It is as if life is put on hold, it stops, until the goal is realized. In the meantime, life passes by and precious moments, never to return, flee quickly with little engagement in the now for what it is.

For the dweller in the past, gratefulness is predicated on what is deemed positive that has already happened; for the inhabitant of tomorrow, gratefulness is conditional. The now is robbed of its sense of grateful joy and celebration. We forget the extraordinary words of Khalil Gibran: "Yesterday is but today's memory and tomorrow is today's dream."[59] To know full gratefulness, the art of living in the present is essential.

To feel grateful is to claim some stake in the joy of living. It suggests the ability to exercise ownership over some piece of life that gives one a feeling of well being and contentment. But taking hold of something you regard as belonging to you, you can create a subtle sense of anxiety. What if I were to lose my precious possession?

The result is an inability to grasp on to gratefulness with some assurance and calm. Instead, we prefer never to feel like rightful owners of our lives. We would rather never to have "loved and lost" than to love and suffer the pain of love lost.

In our society, there is another inhibitor that gets in the way of gratefulness; the subtle yet persuasive feeling that if we truly enjoy what we are and what we have now, we will be obligated later on to pay a heavy price that may not make our current sense of well-being worthwhile. We are convinced that nothing is in fact free; there is a price tag attached to everything. The more I reap a feeling of joy and pleasure from the present, the greater will the price be in the future. Somehow, the cost, in pain or loss, will eventually override the benefit of gratefulness in the here and now. Our thinking is so inextricably tied to the notion of reciprocity that the assumption of unconditional giftedness is alien and highly suspect. Thus we refuse to trust the benign reality of life as it is now and the pleasure and blessing of that which is so readily available to us at the moment. Without paying our dues, we are not entitled to anything. Even the rabbis reiterate this proposition when they state—"le' fum tzara agrah"—the reward is commensurate with the pain.

Psychology or philosophy gives us insight into the difficulty of being grateful or feeling happy. However, biological and physiological factors may contribute as well to our innate sense of unhappiness and ungratefulness. The New Yorker[60] carried an article reviewing several books dealing with the nature of happiness. The article's author claims: "We have been hardwired to emphasize the negative, and for most of human history, there has been a lot of the negative to emphasize." He quotes a behavioral geneticist, David Lykken as saying that "trying to be happier is like trying to be taller."[61]

It is reasonable to speculate that perhaps nature endowed the human with the unyielding sense of dissatisfaction as a way for us to remain vigilant and on guard against the perils of human existence. Discontent and ingratitude help us survive. If the inclination to be unhappy and dissatisfied is a trait with which we are born then we must ask, why expect something different based on a spiritual outlook or perspective on life? If nature dictates ungratefulness, isn't it folly to contradict this powerful propensity? Won't we only invite greater frustration and unhappiness the more we fight our biological and physiological nature?

Within the answer to this question lies the very essence and rationale of religion and spirituality and those ways of life that challenge us to surpass ourselves for the sake of a purpose beyond ourselves. It is religion's claim and task to encourage the human being to rise above nature, to transcend the "God of Nature" and the immutable laws of the natural order and connect to the "God of transcendence," the object of our will and imagination, our intelligence and consciousness, our very spirit and soul.

To cultivate gratefulness is an act of human freedom, which liberates us from the slavery of nature's immutable conclusion that we must be unhappy and ungrateful in order to survive. Gratefulness is an act of defiance in the face of the determinism of the natural law and allows us to roam the recesses of possibility and choice. In this way, gratefulness, in its many expressions and ramifications, paves the way for a spiritual path that can lead us to a life of increased unity with others and growing acts of compassion and loving kindness. The "selfish gene" can be transformed into grateful service.

In sum, gratefulness eludes us if somehow we fail to trust. If flooded with worry and the inability to feel a basic sense of trust about life, one's ability to be grateful, even happy, will remain a human impossibility. To see life as a gift is the sine qua non of joy.

Going Grateful

Recite the following poem several times, and then quietly sit with your eyes closed, thinking of the words.

Today is like every other day, we wake up empty
And frightened. Don't open the door to the study
And begin reading. Take down the dulcimer.
Let the beauty we love be what we do.
There are hundreds of ways to kneel and kiss the ground.
When you go to a garden,
Do you look at horns or flowers?
Spend more time with roses and jasmine.
　　　　　　—Rumi.

Is there something in your life that is your personal and special "dulcimer" for which you are grateful? When you feel empty and frightened, what do you turn to as a source of gratefulness and strength? Write them in your journal; attach them to your scrapbook.

CHAPTER 8

GRATEFULNESS AND SELF

How strange we are in the world, and how presumptuous our doings! Only one response can maintain us: gratefulness for witnessing the wonder, for the gift of our unearned right to serve, to adore, and to fulfill. It is gratefulness which makes the soul great.

Abraham Joshua Heschel [62]

Identity is a highly complex phenomenon. It is not something you see or touch. Rather, it is something that you feel, intuit, imagine, and perceive internally. Its components are many and manifold. It is forged out of experiences and events that transpire from within and without.

In the seventeenth century, Renee Descartes gave the world his famous dictum—"cogito ergo sum"—I think therefore I am. This turning point in the history of Western philosophy made the claim that one's capacity to think, i.e. to doubt, is inescapable proof of one's existence; that the reality of one's existence is born out of the capacity to reason and exercise consciousness of one's thinking and feeling.

If we step away from the abstract and make our way to more tangible criteria, we will encounter a host of other ways by which we assert our identity. For example, I am what I do. One's occupation, profession or source of livelihood determines who one is in the eyes of others and oneself. To the question, "What do you do?", we respond not in kind—we do this or that; rather we answer by saying what we are—"I am a doctor; I am a lawyer; I am a businessman; I am a rabbi!"

A humorous yet pretty serious caption put it this way: "I shop, therefore I am!" The cartoon's relevance lies in its zeroing in on a hallmark of contemporary culture, which is the emphasis on shallow criteria for measuring self-worth and creating identity: "I have, therefore I am!" "I am beautiful, therefore I am!" "I am thin, therefore I am!" "I am powerful, therefore I am!" "I am smart, therefore I am!" "I am famous, therefore I am!" "I win, therefore I am!" "I have more toys, therefore I am!"

These standards have evolved into a national pathology. They have created an environment of anxiety, anger and anguish by establishing the external and material as the exclusive and all-encompassing means for the forging of identity and determining our value to the utter exclusion of the human spirit and its infinite capacity for spiritual regeneration and growth. We seem to invest so much of ourselves and what we hold dear to adding days to our lives, rather than adding life to our days.

What if we strip away all the facades of activity, wealth, possession, celebrity, knowledge and status? Who are we as spiritual beings, in the presence of a God who represents the ultimate, most meaningful and holy in life?

It is generally assumed that our view of the world is determined in large part by our view of ourselves. But isn't it the reverse, that how we understand the nature of and things influences our identities as human beings? Essentially there are three ways by which we can relate to our lives and to the world in general. The first is that the world owes us everything, we are fundamentally entitled, by virtue of our being human, to receive all that we want. A sense of unbridled entitlement is the product of and a contributing psychological factor to the personality of a narcissist.

The second is that all of life is random and accidental, so that whatever one could expect is the result of luck or circumstance, over which we wield little if any control or influence. Seeing life as a consequence of randomness heightens one's self-perception as insignificant and having little if any meaning or responsibility. We owe nothing to the world of today nor to the world of tomorrow. The world of yesterday, with all its generations of benefactors, is an irrelevancy. This perspective is the one of the nihilist.

The third approach, the one I espouse, is that as human beings we are indebted to the source of all life for its countless gifts and stand in wonder and gratefulness for everything and anything that we have and experience. This point of view is one of searching for moral meaning in life and responding to existence through the lens of on-going wonder with an accompanying experience of gratefulness and thanksgiving. This frame of mind, I believe, reflects the posture of the idealistic realist.

Spiritual[63] identity is an identity that is grounded in the soil of gratefulness. The philosopher Soren Kierkegard asserted that thankfulness, a relationship of gratefulness to God and to others, constitutes the person's being. Experiences and expressions of gratefulness thus shape identity.[64]

For me, religion's most essential value lies in its ability to guide us away from narcissism, a natural predisposition of the human condition, and from a life of meaninglessness, to a greater state of altruism and purpose, which represents the challenge, and achievement of our "spiritual" dimension, our consciousness and self-awareness.

We begin our lives in a state of total self-centeredness, perceiving ourselves as the center of the universe. As we mature, the world expands so that others become important parts of that universe-our parents, our siblings, other family members, friends, our ethnic or national group and hopefully, the entire human community. The higher the level of altruism, the greater our sense of maturity.

In other words, loving is a measure of maturity. For Heschel the definition of a human was one who was concerned with others. As he put it," a stone is self-sufficient, man is self-surpassing . . . . man cannot be in accord with his own self unless he serves something beyond himself"[65]. From the perspective of gratefulness, therefore, we can assert that by being grateful we acknowledge the love or "Giving ness" of God, and in the development of this attitude of gratefulness we grow psychologically and spiritually.

A definition of maturity provided by Abraham Maslow, the psychologist who emphasized the hierarchy of needs and the human requirements to have these needs met in order to achieve happiness, is the following: "the ability to appreciate again and again, freshly and naively, the basic goods of life with awe, pleasure, wonder, even ecstasy."

The awareness of self encompasses an overlapping of psychology and spirituality. Who one is as a distinctive entity, an individual apart from others, is arrived at by a myriad of factors. Physiological configuration, temperament, family interactions, school, work, social and cultural settings all represent environments of influence in the evolution of one's sense of self. Essentially, the social framework is the context for the shaping of that which makes us different. As the French sociologist, Alfred Memmi puts it: "To be aware of oneself is to be different. To be is to be different."

It is no mean task to remain true to oneself, cultivate a sense of integrity and not be unduly influenced by the mores of one's society, which may be degrading and demoralizing. As e.e. cummings expressed it: "To be nobody but yourself in a world which is doing its best to make you everybody else, means to fight the hardest battle ever and to never stop fighting."[66]

The mystery of human difference and individuality is beautifully captured in a Mishnah, the code of Rabbinic Jewish Law: "Therefore but a single man was created in the world to proclaim the greatness of the Holy One, blessed be He; for man stamps many coins with one seal and they are all like one another; but the King of Kings has stamped every human with the seal of the first human yet not one is like his fellows."[67]

While one's individuality is the concern of psychology, I would argue that one's spiritual uniqueness is the purview of religion. This sense of inviolability and ultimate worth is derived from a reality that transcends the social, physiological and psychological. The human as irreplaceable is rooted in a transcendent source. The words of the Jewish prayer book recited each morning upon awakening provide the cornerstone for cultivating this spiritual identity." Modeh ani Lefanehcha"-lit. "Thank I before You!"

The recognition of and gratefulness for one's being in the presence of God—being alive—is the raw material out of which an authentic sense of "I" is forged. Soloveitchik states: "A redeemed existence . . . is experienced in the privacy of one's in-depth personality . . . and reaches into the very hidden strata of the isolated "I" who knows himself as a singular being . . . The individual intuits his existence as worthwhile, legitimate and adequate, anchored in something stable and unchangeable."[68] The recitation of thanks in God's Presence who is—"chai v'kayam"-enduring and everlasting, resonates with the grateful awareness of being attached to a stable and unchangeable reality, which confers unique identity upon the individual human soul.

The construct of the human "self"—the part of one's being that is unique and distinctive, representing the integration of characteristics that constitute one's self-awareness as a singular and irreplaceable human entity—is an elusive yet universally recognized idea. According to the point of view that is religiously rooted, the "I", one's authentic identity, is fashioned through awareness of a God that the world reflects and at the same time stands for. Heschel puts it this way: "We begin to understand that what is an "I" to our minds is an "it" to God. This is why object-consciousness rather than self-consciousness is the starting point of our thoughts about God . . . . to think of Him is to open our minds to His all-pervading presence, to our being replete with His presence . . ."[69]

One essential path to the healthy development of one's sense of self is achieved through the cultivation of a sense of gratefulness, by viewing and interpreting the world and life from the perspective of thankfulness and gratitude.

If we return to the opening prayerful words of the day, the "I" is positioned between two other words, "thank"(mode) and "before You,"(lefanecha) in the presence of God. One's sense of self is derived, strengthened and consolidated out of a grateful awareness for all that she or he is and has as a result of recognizing the ultimate Source of these gifts of life, the Ultimate Giver, God. The acknowledgement of oneself as a gift is inherently a perception that leads to a sense of self-worth and value. If at the very foundation of everything is the gift of being, then all things are to be regarded as expressions of "God's" generosity and kindness. Simply put, "I am therefore I thank."

The contemporary Jewish mystic, Rabbi Isaac Kuk, said it well:

> "Every person needs to know
> That he is called to serve
> Based on the model of perception and feeling
> Which is unique to him,
> Based on the core root of his soul.
> In that root,
> Which contains infinite worlds,
> He will find the treasure of his life.
>
> A person needs to say-
> "The world was created for my sake"
> "Bishvily nivrah haolam"[70]

It was two days before my 64th birthday. While jogging, I was suddenly overcome by the desire to run in the next NYC marathon so as to celebrate my 65th birthday in a more challenging and dramatic way. Although a runner for many years, the marathon always seemed way beyond my reach.

Many years before, I had adopted a series of Jewish "mantras'" that I would focus upon as I ran. One was-"EYEH ASHER EYEH"-"I will be what I shall be," the self-definition of God by God to Moses in Exodus 3:14. The breath and the silent articulation of these words reinforced each other and allowed me to jog with a greater sense of freedom and strength. Today my mantra has changed. It is not only a part of the jogging experience but also an integral part of my total spiritual journey. "Modeh ani Lefanehcha"-I thank You. By being grateful for the daily gift of life, I feel that I am—"lefanehcha"-before You, in Your Presence. My mantra alternates between the words "EYEH" and "MODEH", 'I WILL BE, I AM' and "I THANK, I AM GRATEFUL." Thus the connection between my "I" ness and "gratefulness" is reinforced each time I run. The link between gratefulness and "selfness" becomes grounded in the very act of breathing.

The marathon had become not only a desired feat of personal achievement, but had marked the challenge of stretching myself more fully, and with the guidance and impetus of prayerful gratefulness, would perhaps help me complete the breathtaking task of completing the full 26.2 miles of the running course.

Going Grateful

Upon awakening in the morning, remain in bed for a few moments. Set your alarm clock the night before to allow for a few extra minutes in bed, awake and alert to the promise of the day ahead of you.

Repeat the Hebrew word-MODEH, masculine, and MODAH, feminine—I thank. As you repeat the word, smile to yourself. Remain quiet, as the sleepiness of the previous night wears off and in its place rises the feeling of expectation about the day ahead. Breathe slowly and with each in and out breath be mindful of being alive, of being able to breathe, to think, to feel.

In the Eastern tradition of meditation, the sound of "OM' is widely used to connect the mind of the meditator with the ultimate sound of the universe. This sound can be integrated into a gratefulness meditation that incorporates the first two letters of the opening Jewish prayer recited upon awakening-"{MO} DEH-DAH". In fact, the "OM" and the "MO" are simply the reversal of two letters, two sounds. As we breathe in, receiving life's gifts, we may express the sound of the universe in the word "OM," and on the out—breadth, we recite the opening letters of the Hebrew word for "I thank", "MO". Thus this simple meditation contains the very essence of the gratefulness practice. We draw in life from the universe, and respond with gratefulness to this gift.

When you awaken, take your journal and describe what it means to be awake, how it feels, the sensations of being conscious and aware.

Complete the following statements in your journal:

1. I am grateful for being a woman/man because . . .
2. I am grateful for my work or school because . . .
3. I am grateful for my talents and skills—art, music, crafts, dance etc . . .

"Waking up this morning, I smile
Twenty-four brand new hours are before me,
I vow to live fully in each moment
And to look at all beings with eyes of compassion."
Thich Nhat Hanh-*Present Moment, Wonderful Moment*

CHAPTER 9

EVIL AND GRATEFULNESS

*"The whole world lives within a safeguarding, fish
Inside waves, birds held in the sky, the elephant,
The wolf, the lion as he hunts, the dragon, the ant,
The waiting snake, even the ground, the air,
The water, every spark floating up from the fire,
All subsist, exist, and are held in the divine. Nothing
Is ever alone for a single moment.*

*All giving comes from There, No matter who
You think you put your open hand out
Toward, it's That which gives."*

—Rumi

On December 26, 2004, a natural catastrophe of Biblical proportions struck Southeast Asia. In the wake of this tsunami which wiped out over 150,000 lives in a matter of a few short hours, the world was engulfed in one massive tsunami-like philosophical and spiritual conundrum: Why did this happen? How could a compassionate and loving God "allow" so many innocent people to die this way, especially the thousands upon thousands of children? How can we comprehend such callousness in light of the belief in a just and caring God who created the world and who guides it?

Spokespeople of all religious and philosophical persuasions articulated a wide range of opinion. For some, this was a manifestation of God's punishment for behavior seen by some as "evil" and "immoral" such as nudity, promiscuity, and excessive frivolity.

This extreme form of condemnation is unwarranted and spiritually untenable. The innocent victim must never be held morally accountable, and this kind of thinking runs the risk of unjustly blaming the victim. Justice demands commensurability and I strongly suspect that death is not quite a fair punishment for gambling or illicit sexual activity. After all, these locations are lacking in industrial development and their populations can survive only with the infusion of wealth from tourists from abroad. Furthermore, the poor natives are the ones who suffered most while those engaged directly in the so-called immoral activities were more likely to survive the catastrophe. Logic doesn't prevail in the moral equation of western moralists who are so quick to judge and condemn.

Moreover, I prefer to view God not as a source of harsh punishment but rather as the fountainhead of love, compassion and caring.

Others understood this calamity by dividing the world between the natural law which is inexorable and descriptive—what "is"-and human reality over which we can exercise choice, which contains a large measure of the prescriptive-what "ought to be"-obligating us to improve and better our lives.

Closely related to this level of understanding is the view that focuses not upon the cause but on the consequence and its impact on human behavior. The response of the human community is the determining factor in coming to terms with such phenomena of destruction. If human beings rise up with compassion and a renewed sense of unity and humility, then we can catch glimpses of godliness in these responses and interpret the horror of such events as painful but necessary occurrences leading to greater moral and human refinement. In other words, if purposefulness can be extracted from calamity, we can then find an avenue of some solace and comfort.

Such vexing questions have arisen in the human mind since the beginning of time. From the world of Job to the post-Holocaust world, the greatest challenge confronting traditional religious thought lies in the perceived contradiction between the belief in an omnipotent, omniscient and benevolent God and the unmistakable reality of evil and suffering in the world. In simpler and more dramatic terms, this dilemma can be posed as follows: "Why do bad things happen to good people?" This question is considered by many as the central theological question challenging belief in a God of compassion and justice. Perhaps our innate sense of fairness doesn't quite square with the observable events of everyday life which indicate not only unfairness i.e. the good person suffering while the bad person prospers, but also circumstances that reflect a randomness to life, a feeling that things just happen for no apparent or justifiable reason.

Indeed, when we feel we have been unfairly treated or afflicted with some hardship that does not correspond with what we consider to be the natural and expected flow of events i.e. an uncontrollable accident, the premature death of an individual, the death of innocent people due to catastrophic phenomena, "things" going wrong for no good reason, how do we not become subject to overwhelming feelings of anger, envy and fear? How do we retrieve a sense of balance and emotional equanimity when our minds and hearts are flooded with thoughts and feelings that are vengeful or self-punishing, furious and fearful? Even when our lives are calmer, our thinking more rational, do we not contemplate the chaos of life, its messiness, its confusion, its lack of orderliness?

Perhaps the most dramatic expression of this sense of despair and alienation is contained in the passages of Psalm 42.

> *My tears have been my food day and night,*
> *I am taunted with "Where is your God?"*
> *How I walked with the festive crowd . . .*
> *Why so downcast, my soul,*
> *Why disquieted within me . . ." (4-6)*

The Psalmist describes a circumstance of all engrossing dejection in which the company of others who seem to be joyful and festive only exacerbates the feeling of being downcast even more. He cannot shake the disquiet. The one hope of inner spiritual liberation is suggested by the following verse.

> *O my God, my soul is downcast;*
> *Therefore I think of you*
> *In this land of Jordan and Hermon and Mt. Mizar*
> *Where deep calls to deep*
> *In the roar of Your torrents . . .*
> *By day may the Lord vouchsafe His faithful care,*
> *So that a song may be sung in the evening. (7-9)*

The phrase "I think of You" can be translated differently. In Hebrew, the word is "*ezkorcha*", "I will remember You," the root word being "*zachor.*" The Psalmist brings to mind with full awareness the events of glory and celebration associated with the places of Jordan, Hermon and Mt. Mizar, and these enable him to reconnect to the possibility of once again experiencing God's compassion and care and being emotionally capable of praising God with song out of a sense of renewed gratefulness.

One morning, as I was reciting the paragraph on the "Tzitzit"—the tassels that constitute the prayer shawl, instructing us to "look upon the fringes and—"U'zechartem", to remember the Mitzvot, the sacred duties of God, and become Holy unto God"[71], the term "remember"—"Zachor," crystallized in my mind as the internal process by which one can gain an attentive perception and understanding of life's many blessings. The notion of "Zachor"—, highlighted in so many essential contexts of the Bible and Jewish liturgy, suggests a spiritual phenomenon and challenge that goes beyond the mere act of mechanical memory. It is a term that can guide us to the path of greater mindfulness and awareness of the sacredness of the "All" of life and its grandeur, its divinity, its place as a place of God's presence. "Zachor" is a spiritual summons to consider and contemplate the meaning embedded in the mystery of human existence and the vastness of the universe.

This concept isn't limited to Jewish theology. Thich Nhat Hanh, the well-known Vietnamese Buddhist monk, tells a story that plays to the same theme." When I was in Montreal several years ago to lead a retreat, a friend drove me across the city to the mountains. I noticed that every time a car stopped in from of me, the sentence "Je me souviens" was on the license plate. It means—"I remember." I was not sure what they wanted to remember, perhaps their French origins, but I told my friend that I had a gift for him. "Every time you see a car with the sentence, "Je me souviens," remember to breath and smile. It is a bell of mindfulness. You will have many opportunities to breathe and smile as you drive through Montreal." [72]

To remember in Judaism too is like a bell that awakens our mindfulness of the need to be grateful for the goodness and gifts of God to us in our past and as an on-going expression of a loving relationship now and into the future.

Remembering in the sense of deeper awareness is the impetus and inner energy that leads to responses of service and love.

At the heart of every Jewish festival is the formalized ritual of remembering the Exodus from Egypt, especially during Passover. More than simply recalling, each sacred occasion elicits a sense of gratefulness and challenges us to liberate our souls from the spiritual bondage we find ourselves in and to heighten the immediacy of the need for freedom all around us.

Every culture celebrates a new year. Rosh Hashanah, the Jewish New Year is regarded by tradition as the day of remembrance-"Yom Hazikaron". There are absolutely no historical or agricultural connections to this festival as is the case with the pilgrimage festivals of Passover, Succoth and Shavuot. The ritual adornments are sparse. Unlike the festivals of Succoth and Passover, both of which are rich in sensual content—special foods on Passover, the Seder and all its many symbolic items, the Sukkah and the Four Species on Succoth—Rosh Hashanah's objective and experience are entirely spiritual. The individual encounters God nakedly, without external or tangible trappings. The single ritual object used on the festival is the Shofar, the ram's horn, which when sounded evokes memory, recall and mindfulness. All we have is ourselves, our prayers, our ability to "zachor"-to remember, to be mindful and introspective and fully awake to the glory of life, its fleetingness and its impermanence, its beauty and its wonder, its preciousness and precariousness, its opportunity for change and spiritual self-enhancement. On the Jewish New Year we remember to be grateful and to return to a path of greater kindness and compassion.

Not only is this term—"Zachor"—directed to man, but it is also used widely and intentionally in our prayers as we direct our words, thoughts and feelings toward God. We ask God to remember, to be mindful of one fundamental moral and spiritual reality: His nature and essence when relating to us and responding to our prayers—"Remember your compassion, your kindnesses, your "chessed", O Lord, Your tenderness from of old, for they are everlasting."[73] The quality and capacity of God to exercise compassion overpowers His inclination to judge, to be angry or vengeful. The Babylonian Talmud tells us that "Even when the Holy One waxes angry, He remembers i.e. He is mindful, of His mercy"—His compassion and pity, tenderness and kindness, and sensitivity to our frailties and shortcomings.[74] God Himself is, as it were, engaged in a struggle between His absolute power, His Omnipotence that can wreak pain and destruction upon human beings, and His nature of goodness and compassion, which is necessary to allow the world to survive. God Himself, as it were, practices "mindful" contemplation and meditation.

Returning to our Psalm, the conviction that "I will remember You in the land of Jordan and Hermon in Mount Mizar, where deep calls to deep, and the roar of earth's cataracts and the billows and breakers of the waters sweep over me," is the inner pathway from a sense of perdition to praise, a gateway from grief to gratitude and a renewed sense of God's available kindnesses. As we sharpen our awareness of the totality of life, its grandeur, mystery and giftedness, all suggested by the geographical locations referred to by the Psalmist above, our depression may lift and a renewed sense of buoyancy and hopefulness may find its way back into our minds and hearts.

Gratefulness can hold out to us the inner possibility of opening even a tiny space in our wounded and scarred hearts through which some light from the Oneness and love that pulsate through life, the "luminescent enchantment of the created world",[75] can find its way. Again, the Psalmist's words; "I called to the Lord from my narrow prison and He answered me with the freedom of spaciousness."(Chpt.118, v.5)

There are times when in the midst of anguish, encircled by the loss of hope and the constriction of faith and joy, one discovers a simple detail of life, identifies an iota of beauty, one of the myriad, "ordinary" gifts of God, and finds it in his heart to praise.

The Israeli poet Abba Kovner, who invented the idea of Jewish resistance in the Vilna Ghetto during World War II, wrote a soulful book of poems, which he named for the place where he sought survival once again, "'Sloan-Kettering". Kovner writes:

> *"Sloan-Kettering is a large and growing building*
> *And all those who come within its walls*
> *To strip naked,*
> *Jointly and separately,*
> *Suddenly find themselves*
> *In a cage, captive, exposed?*
> *Sloan-Kettering is a personal encounter*
> *With a pathless wilderness!*
> *. . . How little we need*
> *To be happy:*
> *A half-kilo increase in weight,*
> *Two circuits of the corridors*
> *At Sloan-Kettering*
> *In bedroom slippers.*
> *A morning without aspirin*
> *Silence gentle as pit,*
> *A distant*
> *Sand dune*
> *Behind the green bridge*
> *A patch of lawn*
> *And you beside me beginning*
> *To knit a new sweater."*[76]

In no small measure, our misery and disappointments are determined by personal expectations of what in fact could be sources of joy and contentment. In other words, when we are so constricted by narrow desires and wishes that we cannot break this barrier of separateness and isolation, we find ourselves prisoners of our self-serving expectations and aspirations, and gratefulness becomes a reality beyond our reach. It is for this reason that the Sayings of the Sages make the following recommendation: "Rabban Gamliel would say: Do His will as though it were yours, so that He will do your will as if it were His."[77]. Often it is in the seeing of oneself as victim, as target of life's unfairness that engenders a feeling of ingratitude and makes it nearly impossible for a perception of some equilibrium to take hold. To regard oneself as subject to deprivation is to constantly feel cheated and neglected, if not abandoned, by God and life itself. The result is a bottomless space of unfulfilled desires and dreams. By contrast, however, some awareness of the giftedness of life in its totality can provide some sense of acceptance and serenity in the face of life's many trials and challenges. Even in the direst of conditions, most of us can identify something in our lives that sheds its rays of thankfulness upon us—a loved one, a joyful experience or anticipated event, something that made us happy, a gift of some kind freely given. If life can be understood at the core as a gift, as a source of goodness and love extended to all, then there is the possibility of human happiness and the cumulative spiritual strength needed when times are tough and demanding.

When stricken with paralysis, Franz Rosenzweig, the great German-Jewish theologian of the 20th century, once said: "This has been my most memorable experience. As much as has been taken away is given again. This is no law: it can't be reckoned with in advance, and it doesn't free the heart from fear and hope. But afterwards, once it has been experienced, it is an infinite solace and an inexhaustible source of gratitude."[78]

Even when considering the tsunami disaster, scientists were quick to point out something of fundamental importance, which is indispensable for our physical, emotional and moral recovery.

"In the very long view, the global process behind earthquakes is quite advantageous for life on earth-especially human life. Powerful jolts like the one that sent killer waves racing across the Indian Ocean . . . are inevitable side effects of the constant recycling of planetary crust which produces a lush, habitable planet . . . this crystal recycling made the oceans and atmosphere and formed continents . . . . the type of geological process that caused the earthquake and tsunami is an essential characteristic of the earth. As far as we know, it doesn't occur on any other planetary body . . . many biologists believe that this process may have given birth to life itself . . . . there is no question that plate tectonics rejuvenates the planet . . . Nature is reborn with these kinds of terrible events."[79]

Driving along a highway I am often struck by the sight of a flower or a sprig of green sprouting out from between cracks and crevices along the side of a blasted away wall of concrete and rock. No matter how barren and bare a natural surface may be, somehow there lingers a trace of life, of reawakening and renewed growth. Perhaps the unmistakable and undeniable renewability of life is at the heart of all existence and helps us hold on to hope.

The total view of life that acknowledges the "good" that is embedded in the "bad" within the spectrum of "allness" invests and enhances our spiritual capacity to touch gratefulness even at moments of trial and tribulation. Emotionally acknowledging that individual human life issues out of the pain of childbirth helps makes such pain bearable. So too, is all life an emergence out of struggle and suffering for which we can maintain the internal posture of gratefulness and joy.

Gratefulness releases us from the tunnel vision of stress and depression, which constricts our sight to see only difficulty, and problems, helping us widen our vision of life and became aware of the plenitude and bounty that surrounds us.

The first blessing of the formal Morning Prayer concludes with: "He created "Hakol", everything. Through the acceptance of "allness" as the product of God's beneficence, we thank God for His Gift of all, for the totality of everything.

But, the premise of God as the Source of all things also confronts us with the apparent contradiction between God as beneficent and the reality of evil and suffering in the world. If God is the reason for everything, He is also the creator of that which is evil, the cause of so much agony and pain. Interestingly, the Biblical source of this opening blessing is Isaiah 45:7 where the text reads a little differently: "I form light and create darkness, I make weal and create woe."

The Hebrew word for "woe" is "Ra", also meaning evil or bad. With its ascription of "ra", of evil, to God, this passage poses a serious theological challenge. By altering the original text to read: "He created everything", and conveying to the worshiper the perception of the totality, the "allness", of life, the prayer book helps us relate to that which is regarded as "evil" by either making an effort to erase or transform it, or by realizing that the all-embracing quality of life eclipses the reality of evil.

Rabbi Soloveitchik, in the course of interpreting the nature of Jewish prayer, highlights the perspective of "allness" as the spiritual ambience in which evil is absorbed to the point of its near dissolution. He states: "The prayer connects the cosmic order with an ethical category: God is the Creator of light and darkness, the Maker of peace and all things. The word "hakol", "all", means not only the tangible natural phenomena but ethical ideas as well. "Hakol" in this context serves as a substitute for "ra", evil . . . Indeed, the word "hakol" offers an explanation of the phrase "creates evil", in Isaiah. "Ra" is only an illusion, a non-being which one apprehends when beholding only a minute segment of creation . . . Yet, within the greater, all-inclusive perspective, embracing the totality of being, it is part of an organic whole. Evil is dissolved into the universal pattern of goodness . . . Creation is an all-encompassing act."[80]

The ability to surpass psychology and meet the metaphysical is perhaps the most difficult demand of the spiritual life. Is the reality of evil such that it cannot be transcended or transformed? The avenue of gratefulness contributes greatly to this process of self-surpassing and finding our way to touching the transcendent so that "evil is dissolved into the pattern of goodness". By no means do I suggest that evil be ignored or relegated to the world of illusion. On the contrary, gratefulness, which has the power of helping the individual approach evil metaphysically, that is to transcend it and connect to the good, at the same time can become the vehicle for translating the metaphysical into an ethical response of "Chessed," of compassion and love.

A slogan of the ecology movement is particularly apt. "Think globally; act locally." The metaphysics of gratefulness allows us to perceive the "allness" of life and thus bring a perspective of greater serenity into our hearts. The ethics of gratefulness engender a response of compassion and care into the immediate orbit of our daily lives.

Abraham, the founder of the Jewish faith, emerges according to Jewish tradition as the embodiment of the spiritual characteristic of compassion and loving-kindness. This singular definition of his spiritual identity can be associated with one particular verse, which describes his understanding of reality toward the end of his life. "And God blessed Abraham—"Bakol"—in all things or with everything."[81] What was the need to add "everything" if the obvious implication of blessing is precisely that, in which case the text could have read: "And God blessed Abraham!" The word "bakol"-with everything, seems superfluous. Nachmanides, the great 13th century exegete, understands this verse to mean that Abraham was blessed with the divine attribute of "allness." That is, the ability to perceive "allness" is a way of comprehending the divine, and coping with evil and suffering. Furthermore, this internal cognition finds its natural external expression in acts of "chessed", in relating to others, to oneself and to the entire world of God's creation, with compassion and kindness.[82] In light of this passage occurring immediately after the death of Abraham's wife, Sarah, the notion of God's blessing of "allness" takes on a particular poignancy. [83]

If one understands all of life as a gift from a Divine Source, what other way is there for us to respond if not with compassion, generosity and love? To be compassionate to all of life is to be godly, to share in God's understanding of the meaning and purpose of life. It is this particular perspective that accounts for Abraham's extraordinary relationship with God. The broader one's view of life, taking in its many wonders and diversities, grandeur and vastness, the more successfully can one cope with life's sorrows and suffering.

The book of Job is the quintessential statement of challenge to the notion of goodness and fairness in the face of unjustified and unexplainable suffering and pain. After undergoing intolerable loss of possessions and family, and being stricken himself for no apparent reason, Job struggles to understand the meaning of evil in light of his goodness and righteousness. Only at the very end of the book, when God speaks to him out of the whirlwind in chapters 38-41,emphasizing the inexplicable wonder and grandeur of God's creation, does Job arrive at a profound realization of God's reality as he says: "But now I see You with my eyes."(Chpt. 42: V.5) Susan Neiman, in *Moral Clarity*, phrases this spiritual insight of Job in these words:" Genesis merely tells us that it (the Creation)" was very good:" here (in the speech out of the Whirlwind) it is great and teeming . . . Life itself is a gift, when this is what it looks like and each one of us is in debt to the world for the gift of having lived in it."

The experience of evil in the presence of a benevolent God nonetheless persists as a mystery. Perhaps it is the "mysterious" that must become our final refuge by which to reconcile ourselves with its intractability and incomprehensibility, and yet maintain our attitude of gratefulness for the totality of life. What do we do in the face of a God who is often experienced as a "deus absconditus", an absent God, whose "far-away ness" frightens us and leaves us feeling so vulnerable, even abandoned?

Robert Fulghum, in a delightfully entertaining yet instructive way, shares his philosophy of life in a charming book called-*All I Really Need to Know I learned in Kindergarten*. One of his very perceptive understandings of God is related through the use of a child's game.

"Better than hide-and-seek, I like the game called Sardines. In Sardines, the person who is it goes and hides, and everybody goes looking for him. When you find him you get in with him and hide there with him. Pretty soon everybody is hiding together, all stacked in a small space like puppies in a pile. And pretty soon somebody giggles and somebody laughs and everybody gets found ... medieval theologians even described God in hide-and-seek terms, calling Him Deus Absconditus. But me, I think old God is a sardine player. And will be found the same way everybody gets found in Sardines-by the sound of laughter of those heaped together at the end."[84]

Life is filled with the unknown and the unexplainable. Rachel Naomi Remen sees this in positive terms of mystery: "Life is neither linear nor is it stagnant. It is movement from mystery to mystery."[85] She goes on: "Mystery seems to have the power to comfort, to offer hope, and to lend meaning in times of loss and pain. In surprising ways, it is the mysterious that strengthens us at such times ... I now offer my companionship and share my sense of mystery, of the possible, of the wonder."[86]

To accept the mystery of life, the overwhelming reality of the "awesome" and "marvelous", is to recognize an answer, which may not be able to explain anything except the reality of life's totality and "allness."

The great scientist of the 20th century, Albert Einstein, also spoke of God as mystery. "The most beautiful and deepest experience one can have is the sense of mysterious ... To sense that behind anything that can be experienced there is something that our mind cannot grasp and whose beauty and sublimity reaches us only indirectly and as a feeble reflection, this is religiousness. In this sense, I am religious."[87]

In times of challenge, the person of gratefulness can see her way clear to thank God not for the loss, hardship or suffering of the moment, but rather for the gift of realizing the mystery of life, the totality of life and the capacity to accept this mystery without guilt, self-blame or recrimination.

Mystery is not limited to the transcendent dimension of God or to those phenomena for which rational explanations are not readily available. Mystery is contained in the very immanence of God's many manifestations. To the grateful heart the world is a place of great mystery.

The energy of life that courses through the universe is at one and the same time an expression of praise and the melody of life's miracle.

There are times, however, when our ability to be grateful is next to impossible. We feel a powerful blockage or obstacle, as if the spiritual arteries of our hearts were clogged, so that the blood of blessing simply cannot get through, and those precious channels of feeling and connection are filled with the plaque of some impediment that leaves us frightened and alone.

Often, when praying, I find myself confronted by a wide disparity between the words that I read and my experience of the world around me, between what I say and what I feel. God as Giver remains an abstraction rather than an intimate intuition of inner clarity that informs my life and inspires a sense of gratefulness.

When we feel hopeless, numb or confused, God's "chessed", divine nurturance seems beyond our grasp, so very far away, "beyond the sea and high in the sky"-and we are left feeling alone and abandoned. God is absent because His "Chessed"—His compassion appears unreal, a cruel hoax, even a lie. It is at a time such as this that the mindful awareness of the "allness" of life, no matter how dim against the backdrop of so much darkness, can be summoned forth in our souls. Like a droplet of water sliding down a windowpane, the distant echo of gratefulness can slowly, almost imperceptibly, spread its subtle strength to offer a perspective of renewed possibility and promise.

It goes without saying that the power of this awareness is greatly increased and more naturally accessible if one incorporates a gratefulness practice in everyday life. Over time, this view of life has the potential to neutralize and offset the emotional and spiritual devastation that may accompany a sudden experience of suffering and setback. At such a time, the words of the great poet of Israel, Leah Goldberg, come to mind:

> *"Teach me my, God, blessing and prayer-*
> *for the secret of the withered leaf,*
> *the brightness of the ripened fruit*
>
> *For this freedom to see,*
> *To sense, to breathe,*
> *To know, to wish, to fail.*
>
> *Teach my lips a blessing, a song of praise*
> *In renewal of your day*
> *Each morning and eve.*
> *That my today not be like all my yesterdays;"*[88]

Another challenge to our capacity to thank and praise is the reality of change and the impermanent nature of the world. Change frightens us and knowing that life is so unpredictable and uncertain instills our hearts with foreboding.

Yet, Jewish prayer celebrates change and renewal. The morning service continues: "Hamechadesh B'tuvo b'chol yom tamid maasei breshit"-"He renews creation each and every day in His goodness."[89]

Every day is different from the previous one and represents a source of renewal and change, considered by Jewish thought as being "good," an act of God's essence, and His creative compassion. Without change and renewal, without the pulse of life in all its countless forms, all would remain static and stale. The impermanence of life is not a reality of which we should be frightened, but a fundamental gift for which we can and should be grateful.

The Rabbis proclaim that every miniscule particle of life is reason for blessing. "What blessing should one say [for rain]? Rabbi Judah taught: We give thanks unto You for every drop You caused to fall on us."[90] Moreover, even those aspects of life that contain moral risk are considered as outgrowths of God's presence and as such warrant blessing." It happened once that Rabban Gamliel saw a beautiful gentile woman, he uttered a blessing at the sight of her . . . was it Rabban Gamliel's habit to gaze at women? No, but the road was torturous and he looked at her without intending to."[91]

The blessing is the briefest way to say "thank you" for the reality of creation and all of life that flows from it.

In one Midrash, we are told that when the letters of the Hebrew alphabet had learned about God's intention to create the world, each letter presented its justification to have the Torah begin with it. Contentiousness among the letters erupted. Finally, the second letter, "Bet," Approached God and said, "Lord of the Universe. May it be Your will to create the world with me-the letter "bet." Indeed, replied the Holy One, I will create the world with you for with you shall all future generations bless Me. (The 'bet' begins the word "baruch," blessed or praised . . . and the Torah begins with: "Bereshit barah Elohim . . ." "In the beginning God created . . ." [92]

Punctuating the passage of time is the on-going regularity of recurring activities that could elicit a response of blessing thereby transforming these "bland" moments into gifts of gratefulness. For the fortunate few, the most commonplace can become a sacred event for which to be profoundly grateful and joyful. In fact, however, the ordinary is an on-going gift for which we can cultivate gratefulness and in this way experience the extraordinary embedded in the ordinary. This discovery of holiness in daily life is described by Holly Bridges Elliot, in *Beholding God in Many Faces:* "I remember this illumination happening to me one noontime as I stood in the kitchen and watched my children eat peanut butter and jelly sandwiches. We were having a most unremarkable time on a nondescript day, in the midst of the most quotidian of routines. I hadn't censed the table, sprinkled the place mats with holy water or uttered a sanctifying prayer over the Wonder bread. I wasn't feeling particularly 'spiritual'. But, heeding I don't know what prompting, I stopped abruptly in mid-bustle, or mid-woolgathering, and looked around me as if I were opening my eyes for the first time that day. The entire room became luminous and so alive with movement that everything seemed suspended-yet pulsating-for an instant, like light waves. Intense joy swelled inside me, and my immediate response was gratitude-gratitude for everything, for every tiny thing in that space. The shelter of the room became a warm embrace; water flowing from the tap seemed a tremendous miracle; and my children became, for a moment, not my progeny or my charges or my tasks, but eternal beings of infinite singularity and complexity whom I would one day, in an age to come, apprehend in their splendid fullness."[93]

Going Grateful

Bring to your mind's eye a difficult moment in your life ie. illness, loss, death. Think about some aspect of that experience that eventually brought you comfort for which you were grateful-the care of a nurse or family member, the support of a friend.

Say "thank you" in your heart for these sources of gratefulness.

Take your journal and record an event of particular challenge to you or a loved one. Describe the aspects of this challenge that were life-enhancing for which you could be thankful.

Whenever you encounter something that you consider as not good in your life, ask yourself? "Is there anything right about what happened?" You need not deny the reality of the bad; rather, try and focus on anything that can be understood as positive and good from the experience.

Before retiring, while lying in bed or sitting quietly we can connect to feelings of gratefulness as we review our day. Again, preparations before bed are rich in potential possibilities that elicit gratefulness awareness. Review your day. Recall one experience or event for which you can feel grateful. Meditate on that moment of gratefulness.

The fact that we sleep is an amazing reality without which we cannot live. To feel refreshed and energetic, even alive, sleep is indispensable. Recite: BLESSED ARE YOU WHO CASTS BONDS OF SLEEP UPON MY EYES AND SLUMBER UPON MY EYELIDS or I AM THANKFUL FOR THE GIFT OF SLEEP THAT REFRESHES MY BODY AND MY SPIRIT.

CHAPTER 10

GRATEFULNESS-A UNIVERSAL GIFT

Travelers fan out
Into the wilds,
And in that jungle
Of strangers
Merci
Rings out
While the hustling train
Changes countries,
Sweeping away borders.
Then spasibo
Clinging to pointy
Volcanoes, to fire and freezing cold,
Or danke, yes! And gracias, *and*
The world turns into a table:
A single word has wiped it clean,
Plates and glasses gleam.
Silverware tinkles,
And the tablecloth is as broad as a plain.
            Pablo Neruda.

All theistic religions presuppose a spiritual posture of gratefulness among their adherents. If God is benevolent, the response of all believers would have to be one of being grateful. Moreover, ideologies and philosophies that are non-theistic ie. Buddhism, secularism, likewise acknowledges the centrality of gratefulness as a virtue that is indispensable to human spiritual growth and betterment. Although not an expert in all religions, I would like to share a brief sketch of some major religious orientations and the outlook of those who view the world from a secular perspective, in the hope of conveying the universality of this concept and helping the reader of whatever persuasion to locate his/her connection to gratefulness from the personal attachment to a formal faith or spiritual frame of reference.

Christianity

A fundamental assumption of Christianity, one shared with Judaism and Islam, is that everything comes from God and that everything, since its source is divine, must be good. While not everything appears to be good to the natural mind, certainly not sin, in essence all must be good if all derives from God. Given this fact of faith, the Christian is expected to respond with gratefulness for all things.

Yet there is evil in the world and the Christian is poignantly aware of the reality of sin. How then does a Christian remain grateful in the presence of sin's persistence? The core of Christian faith is unwaveringly predicated on the belief that God gave His only Son to humanity and that this Son was crucified and served as atonement for the sins of the entire world. What allows the Christian to experience gratefulness even in the face of evil and sorrow is the recognition that Jesus Christ died for humanity's sins and that his resurrection will assure the believer of eternal life.

For Christians, human beings are essentially debtors, not only to God but also to fellow human beings. Human nature is regarded as weak and dependent and Christian tradition makes a virtue of acknowledging human status as recipients, thus reinforcing the inclination to be grateful.

Perhaps the quality of gratefulness as intrinsic to Christian life can be summarized in the following liturgical selection:

Almighty God, Father of all mercies,
We thine unworthy servants
Do give thee most humble and hearty thanks
For all thy goodness and loving-kindness
To us and to all men.

We bless thee for our creation, preservation,
And all the blessings of this life;
But above all for thine inestimable love

In the redemption of the world by our Lord Jesus Christ,
For the means of grace, and for the hope of glory
—Prayer of General Thanksgiving of
the Episcopal *Book of Common Prayer (1979)*

All Christians build into their services a structured time for prayer and Thanksgiving to God. In the *Lutheran Book of Worship*, the minister enunciates what is called "the Great Thanksgiving:"

> Minister: The Lord be with you.
> Congregation: and also with you.
> Minister: Lift up your hearts.
> Congregation: We lift them to the Lord.
> Minister: Let us give thanks to the Lord our God
> Congregation: It is right to give him thanks and praise.
> Minister: It is indeed right and salutary that we should at all times and in all places offer thanks to the Lord.

What follows is the story of what all Christians should be thankful for: that God "filled all creation with light and life, for example, that" through Abraham you promised to bless all nations," that "at the end of all ages you sent your Son, who in words and deeds proclaimed your kingdom, was obedient to your will, even to giving his life."

The ultimate Christian message therefore is be thankful.

A concomitant belief in Protestantism in particular is the awareness of Grace by which one can accept Christ's love. Entering the Kingdom of God is all about the justification by faith through grace. Grace and gratitude spring from the same Latin root, gratus. For God and for human beings, accepting gifts and giving thanks are to be among the most pleasing of human endeavors. (Psychology of Gratitude, P. 85)

Islam

"In the Name of God, the Compassionate Source of All Mercy.
All Praise, the Lord of all worlds, the Compassionate Source of All Mercy
And Master of the Day of Judgment.
You alone do we serve and it is to You alone that we look for help.
Guide us on the Straight Path . . ."

(The Koran 1:1-7)

The holy book of Muslims, the Koran, begins with the recognition of a God who is One and Compassionate. Like Judaism and Christianity, Islam is a monotheistic faith in the extreme, allowing for no visual, tangible or conceptual ideation of God's reality. From the perspective of gratefulness, Islam's emphasis on God as Creator and Source of Compassion is overwhelmingly significant . . . . "it is in the nature of the good to give of itself, and the Infinitely-Good, God, could not but radiate that reality that constitutes the world, in fact, all worlds."[94]

Islam has a system of rituals and practices designed to translate religious belief into reality. This system is called the *Arkan al Islami,* the Pillars of Islam.

1. Shahadah-Declaring allegiance to God
2. Salat-Daily Prayer
3. Zakat-Annul charity
4. Saum-Month long fasting
5. Hajj-Pilgrimage to Mecca.

Each concrete expression of Islamic beliefs reflects a response of gratefulness and thanksgiving from their adherents. One could interpret the first pillar, acknowledging God as Compassionate, as a response of the intellect. The second and fifth pillar, prayer and pilgrimage as a response of the heart. The giving of charity, the third pillar, represents the stretching of the hand in an act of reciprocity and giving for the gifts one receives from the Compassionate Source. And finally the Suam, the month long fast, is a demonstration of a total body response of gratitude in abstaining from food as a gesture of sacrificial gratefulness. The pilgrimage can be added to the experience of comprehensive immersion in the experience of expressing gratefulness for God's blessings.

The Koran, like the Jewish and Christian bibles, recognizes God as the Creator of the world and especially of the human being. In language reminiscent of Genesis, chpt.2: 7, the Koran informs the Muslim of God's gift of creation and existence, bemoaning the fact that humans are "seldom thankful."

"*He first created man from clay and then made his offspring from a drop of humble fluid. He molded him and breathed His spirit into him. He gave you ears and eyes and hearts, yet you are seldom thankful."(The* Koran, 32:7-9).

It is evident that God expects a response of gratefulness for humans considering the ultimate gift of life and existence that originates with God, the ultimate Giver.

Moreover, the Koran urges its adherents to be grateful and articulate thanks for this act of praise and gratitude is one that God desires.

"*If you are thankful, your thanks will please Him.*" (The Koran, 39:39).

From the perspective of the Koran, all of life and its unfolding are in the hands of God. Thus, whenever one is delivered from mishap, it is incumbent upon the rescued individual to give thanks, to express gratefulness. If not, his ingratitude becomes a source of unhappiness and disappointment to God. Ingratitude is equivalent to faithlessness.

"*When at sea a misfortune befalls you, all but Him of those to whom you pray forsake you; yet, when He brings safe to dry land you turn your backs upon Him Truly, man is ever thankless.*"(The Koran 17:67).

Buddhism

"If the absence of a personal Creator-God is atheism, then Buddhism is atheistic."[95]However, the concept of Nirvana, as "*permanent, stable, imperishable, immovable, ageless, deathless, unborn, and unbecome, that is power, bliss and happiness, the secure refuge, the shelter, and the place of unassailable safety; that is the real Truth and the supreme Reality; that is the Good, the supreme goal and the one and only consummation of our life, the eternal, hidden and incomprehensible Peace,*"[96]suggests some notion of Godhead.

Implied in the concept of nirvana, as a spiritual state one strives for, as a living reality, is the presupposition of the experience of gratefulness for any level of attainment of the blessings of nirvana.

Buddhism understanding of life's realities and its "program" of spiritual response are contained in the four most considered convictions about life-THE FOUR NOBLE TRUTHS—and the prescribed course of action to achieve nirvana in the EIGHTFOLD PATH.

Briefly, the Four Noble Truths are:

1. Life is dukkha, *"suffering."*
2. The cause of life's dislocation is *tanha, "desire."*
3. Overcoming selfish craving is to overcome life's dislocation
4. The way of curing these ills is by the Eightfold Path.

THE EIGHTFOLD PATH:

1. Right views-an intellectual response based on reason.
2. Right intent-an emotional response based on the feelings of the heart.

3. Right Speech-proper attention to language
4. Right conduct: understanding behavior and responding to it.
5. Right livelihood: The proper use of most of our time involved in securing a source of income is essential in gaining the objective of spiritual fulfillment.
6. Right effort: Recognition of human will as a basic component in the process of overcoming suffering in life.
7. Right mindfulness
8. Right concentration

The final two paths represent the pivotal way of Buddhist practice, namely the way of meditation. Examining the present mind is fundamental to the spiritual process of arriving at ultimate peace and bliss.

It becomes clear that according to Buddhism, a basic reason for life's unhappiness and sorrow lies in the craving and desires of the human heart. In other words the spiritual poison of life is ingratitude, the chronic condition of excessive dissatisfaction. Suffering results form this attachment to the world; the inaccurate thinking that having and owning bring peace and happiness.

Another central concept is that referred to as *anicca, impermanence*, transitoriness. To desire is to fall prey to the mistaken notion that there are things in life that are permanent and everlasting. A challenge to our capacity to thank and praise is the reality of change and the impermanent nature of the world. From the earliest Greek philosophers such as Heraclitus, to Buddhist thinkers of yesterday and today, the principle of change and impermanence is viewed as an underlying principle by which all of life can be understood. It is difficult at times to accept the reality of change. The prospect of change and impermanence elicits a sense of insecurity leading us to remain where we are or to hope for situations that are stable and unchanging.

The well-known Buddhist monk Thich Nhat Hahn, provides us with the following important perspective on change. "We are often sad and suffer a lot when things change, but change and impermanence have a positive side. Thanks to impermanence, everything is possible. Life itself is possible . . . if your daughter is not impermanent, she cannot grow up to become a woman. Then your grandchildren would never manifest. So instead of complaining about impermanence, we should say, "warm welcome and long live impermanence." We should be happy. When we see the miracle of impermanence, our sadness and suffering will pass."[97]

Gratefulness emerges as a full-fledged characteristic in Buddhism, a natural and necessary outflow of its precepts and practices. *In Buddhism, An*

Introduction, by Huston Smith and Philip Novak, an anonymous Zen teacher describes the feelings that come over one for whom the dissolution of dualism and possessiveness takes place as the following:

"*Infinite gratitude to all things past,*
Infinite service to all things present,
Infinite responsibility to all things future."

Thus, gratefulness emerges as the soil out of which the possibility of service, a moral response of goodness, and responsibility, the recognition of one's moral role in the well being of life, all grow and thrive.

Secularism

For those with a strong formal religious orientation toward life, the notion of a secularist feeling grateful may be difficult to conceive. How do secularists experience gratefulness? If one does not believe in God, then how can one be grateful for one's life and its blessings? To whom can one be grateful?

In the Introduction to "Psychology of Gratitude," Robert C. Solomon asserts:

> "Gratitude is a philosophical emotion . . . It is . . . seeing the bigger picture . . . opening one's heart to the universe is not so much personifying the universe as opening one's heart, that is, expanding one's perspective . . . being grateful for one's life is not a 'grateful to whom?' question so much as it is a matter of *being aware* of one's whole life . . . one recognizes how much of life is out of our hands, how indebted one is or should be to parents, friends, and teachers . . . it is gratitude and humility . . . that form a natural pair."[98]

Moreover, a distinction can be made between transpersonal gratitude and a gratefulness that is grounded in a theistic position. One's gratefulness may be directed to the cosmos in general or to an all-embracing totality of life that transcends one's immediate and constrictive surroundings. "In this attitude people recognize that they are connected to each other in a mysterious and miraculous way that is not fully determined by physical forces, but as part of a wider, or transcendent context."[99] Rabbi Abraham Joshua Heschel, a religious spokesman, poetically put it in a way that resonates with everyone of spiritual inclination: "The insights of wonder must be constantly kept alive. Since there is a need for daily wonder, there is a need for daily worship . . . This is one of the goals of the Jewish way of living: to experience commonplace deeds as spiritual adventures, to feel the hidden love and wisdom in all things."[100]

In spite of his absolute rejection of any form of purposeful design in the universe, even an ardent atheist as Richard Dawkins could nonetheless acknowledge the wonder and sense of astonishment toward life as a gift: "I tried to convey how lucky we are to be alive, given that the vast majority of people who could potentially be thrown up by the combinational lottery of DNA will in fact never be born . . . we are staggeringly lucky to find ourselves in the spotlight. However brief our time in the sun, if we waste a second of it, or complain that it is dull or barren or boring, couldn't this be seen as a callous insult to those trillions who will never even been offered life in the first place?"[101] This statement is an eloquent articulation of a brilliant scientist for whom gratefulness is a necessary human emotional need and an expression of an ethical sensitivity to life.

From the perspective of evolutionary theory, Richard Dawkins goes on to say, " . . . human beings have evolved to exhibit such sympathy-related traits as attachment and cognitive empathy, to establish and respect prescriptive social rules, to reciprocate in kind and to engage in behaviors and to formulate strategies that promote getting along with each other . . . Acts of gratitude are well designed to affirm episodes of reciprocity in social life . . . . indeed, anything that promotes pleasing exchanges between human beings is likely to promote the social good . . ."[102]

Another secularist, scientific view of life, that of psychoanalysis, understands gratefulness as closely tied in to the ability to love. Melanie Klein, a student of Freud, acknowledged "Gratitude is essential to building up the relation to the good object and underlies also the appreciation of goodness in others and in oneself . . . A full gratification at the breast means that the infant feels he has received from his loved object a unique gift that he wants to keep. This is the basis of gratitude. Gratitude is closely linked with the trust in good figures . . ."[103]

A perspective that can be easily shared by both believers and secularists in term of the experience of gratefulness is that of seeing life and the world in its totality and "allness." This view allows us to transcend the narrowness of the immediate moment and place and consider the overarching wonder of all things.

One of the finest expressions of the awareness of the "allness" of life as a source of comfort and hope was articulated by an arch atheist, Robert Ingersoll, during his eulogy for Walt Whitman, March 30, 1892. These were some of his words: "He was the poet of death. He accepted all life and all death, and he justified all. He had the courage to meet all, and was great enough and splendid enough to harmonize all and to accept all there is of life as a divine melody."[104] I believe that the strength to see life in this manner can be derived from an elevated consciousness of gratefulness connected to an underlying conviction that at the heart of all things is in fact a Giver.

Two days before, I had run about eighteen miles as part of my training for the NYC Marathon. Impatient and foolish, I tried the same distance that day. After ten miles, I collapsed. The heat had sucked every drop of energy from my bones. I was dehydrated and no amount of liquid would restore my strength. I sat by the side of the country road, aching, trembling, frightened and alone. Cars whizzed by. I held out my hand, begging for a ride. A truck pulled over. I was barely able to climb into the cab. The driver, sincere and caring, urged me to return home, take a hot bath and take in as many liquids as possible. Reassuring and friendly, he drove on. We arrived at my parked car, and I bid farewell to my savior stranger.

> *No matter what the grief, its weight,*
> *We are obliged to carry it.*
> *We rise and gather momentum, the dull strength*
> *That pushes us through crowd . . .*
> *All day it continues, each kindness*
> *Reaching toward another-a stranger*
> *Singing to no one as I pass on the path . . .*
> Dorianne Laux

CHAPTER 11

MAKING GRATEFULNESS A PART OF YOUR LIFE: A JEWISH APPROACH

Apart from a rare moment of "grace", how does one allow gratefulness to become a pivotal part of one's spiritual life?

Judaism's path toward gratefulness is a three-pronged one and has its source in a statement of the Ethics of the Fathers, or Sayings of the Sages, an ancient text of the Mishnah, redacted circa 200 CE, a work that articulates aphorisms of the rabbis highlighting the basic virtues of moral and spiritual life.

"Simon the Just used to say: The world stands on three things—Torah, Worship and Deeds of loving kindness." [105]

One can understand these three pillars as corresponding to the three human capacities of the mind, the heart and the hand—the intellect being served by the pursuit of Torah, the emotions reaching out to God in worship and the actions of human beings in translating the intangible into acts of goodness and compassion.

I would prefer to consider these three arenas of spiritual quest as overlapping and inseparable so that all parts of the process can be simultaneously engaged as we try to achieve authentic spiritual fulfillment. The study of Torah transcends the intellect; prayer is more than emotion and feeling; and compassion embraces not only the hand but the heart and mind as well.

TORAH

My work is loving the world . . .
Let me keep my mind on what matters

Which is my work,
Which is mostly standing still and learning to be astonished
The phoebe, the delphinium.
The sheep in the pasture, and the pasture.
Which is mostly rejoicing, since all the ingredients are here,
Which is gratitude, to be given a mind and a heart
And these body-clothes,
A mouth with which to give shouts of joy
To the moth and the wren . . .
Telling them all, over and over, how it is
That we live forever [106]

—Mary Oliver

For one to discover gratefulness, Judaism insists on a path of spiritual vitality, which often precedes prayer, and that is Torah. Narrowly defined, Torah refers to the Five Books of Moses. More broadly, it encompasses the entire gamut of Jewish religious literature and lore. To me, Torah represents the Jewish approach to spiritual enlightenment, not merely the contents of a particular book or tradition. The way of Torah is that which leads to a deeper awareness of the miraculous in life, a path that points to a divine source and a gateway to gratefulness.

The Rabbis say: "There are seventy aspects or dimensions to Torah"-the number seventy corresponding to the nations of the world in ancient time.[107] Inherent in the Torah is the totality of wisdom from which all nations and individuals can derive enlightenment, and this infinite potential for such wisdom is contained within the Torah itself.

The word "Torah" has a multiplicity of rich and seminally meaningful word cognates that shed light on its fullest implications. One Hebrew word, in terms of its sound, is not only linguistically connected to Torah but contains philosophical and theological ties as well "OR," light. A Rabbinic exegesis on the Creation of the world suggests that the Torah is eternal and preceded Creation, and that God Himself referred to it as an architect refers to a blueprint when he builds an edifice, without which the structure cannot be built. (Genesis Rabbah 1:1). It is from this source, "T [OR] AH" that one extracts enlightenment, "OR", the light of insight and wisdom.

What is equally fascinating, is that the Source of Torah, God, is perceived by children from around the world with their innocent yet rich imagination, as light.

In attempting to gauge the spiritual feelings of children, Robert J. Landry interviewed children from a wide spectrum of religious traditions. These are some of their responses:

"God is a ray of light that shows us the good way:" Lihi, 10 years old, Jewish, Israel.

"No one can see the real God. But I see really, really bright lights:" Sahar, 8 years old, Muslim, Pakistan.

"One day a large mass of kindness, love and light by the name of God saw the empty, dark world spinning in its orbit with not a spot of light. How much the world needs sunshine to brighten up its sky? So he took his light and made the sun so it wasn't dark anymore:" Francesca, 13 years old, Bahai, USA.[108]

Another linguistic correlation is that which conveys the idea of giving birth and creating life. The root of the Hebrew word for becoming impregnated is "Haroh". Again, this word is closely linked with the word for instruction—"Yaroh"; the word for teacher-"Moreh"-"Morah" (fem.), and "parent" which is "Horeh".

Additionally, the Hebrew word for early rain is "Yoreh", again connected to the Torah's intrinsic quality of life-giving power.

The rabbis make it abundantly clear that the spiritual enterprise embedded in Torah is not only a gift to Israel but to the entire world. "Rabbi Jonathan says: Three things were given as a gift to the world: Torah, the luminaries and rain . . . The Sages add: Also compassion."[109] Again, as light, the luminaries, and rain, are obvious and indispensable gifts to all of humankind, likewise is Torah, or the capacity to gain a spiritual and moral perspective necessary as a foundation for the entire world. The addition of "compassion" as a gift to all is inherent in the nature of both God and the universe.

As a sublime gift of the spirit, its acquisition and incorporation in the life of the individual require recognition of gratefulness to the Ultimate Giver.

Torah is also derived from yet another root word—"YAROH"—which means "to shoot", "to aim", "to focus upon," in order to hit a target. In other words, Torah or instruction is meant to impart something that is accurate and true, a clear message of the mind and heart. To know the wisdom of Torah it is necessary, as the word Torah implies in terms of "aiming" and "focusing upon", to devote mindful attentiveness to sacred words in a way by which we can gain an awareness of God's reality everywhere.

The study of Torah can be understood as a unique form of Jewish mindfulness, the spiritual exercise of an open mind and heart. When studying

Torah, the expectation of our Sages was considerably deeper than the mere intellectual knowledge of the text, in spite of the latter's obvious importance. The purpose of Torah was to engage not only the mind but the heart as well. The grandson of the Besht, the founder of Hassidism, R. Baruch of Medzibezh, describes the study of Torah in the following way:

"The principle is that everyone has first to hear in his heart . . . and afterwards to study what the heart is hearing . . . and this is the meaning of the Torah that is studied for its own sake, to illumine in the Torah what he has heard in his heart . . . and if he did so, then the Torah will illumine in his soul, and this is the meaning of the dictum 'the Holy One, blessed be He, and the Torah and Israel are one.'"[110]

Torah as discipline, practice, and a way of life in the pursuit of the sacred is directed not only at rational thought and logic, but commands the attention of one's intuition as well, or one's soul, a deeper source of cognition that has its place in human creativity, imagination, poetry and the recesses of that part of us that is vital to our moral and spiritual understanding. In the Kabbalistic universe of discourse, the world of Jewish mysticism, the ultimate goal of Torah study as an act of fullest spiritual engagement is to become one with the divine.

A great mathematician, Poincare, understood that "it is by logic that we prove; it is by intuition that we discover."[111] The spiritual pursuit transcends the intellectual need to exercise rational thinking to prove God or the meaning of life. The spiritual enterprise that seeks meaning and value is subject to an inner world that goes beyond one's ability to think. Thus the term used in Hebrew regarding the engagement in Torah is significantly broader than the exercise of study, which in Hebrew is translated as "Talmud Torah". The fuller meaning of Torah "study "is captured in the term-"La-asok"-to engage in, "to busy" oneself with, fully and mindfully, with a commitment to discover the moral and spiritual truth about the reality of life, to discover God. Gratefulness is an indispensable component of this spiritual discovery.

To better understand the process of mindfulness, insight can be garnered from other disciplines and traditions. A psychologist and teacher of meditation, recognized in the medical establishment as providing important techniques and resources for the reduction of human stress, Jon Kabat-Zinn, writes the following definition of mindfulness: "Mindfulness practice provides an opportunity to walk along the path of your own life with your eyes open, awake instead of half unconscious, responding consciously in the world instead of reacting automatically, mindlessly . . . . Rather than a philosophy, it is a way of being, a way of living your moments and living them fully."[112]

Meditation is popularly seen by the general public and health workers as a non-toxic way by which to reduce stress, which results in both physical and psychological benefits. Spiritually, meditation is a technique or discipline that helps one to discover a place or a more expanded space in the mind and heart for the world of the spirit. Usually our minds are flooded with the mental "dross" of everyday life, the worries and concerns of ordinary living which often elicit fantasies, anger and fear. Through the process of meditation, we empty our minds of the concerns of "this" world, which in Kabbalah, Jewish mysticism, is defined as "olam ha-asiyah"—"the world of "doing" or "activity", that requires ego-identity, ambition and drive and desire to succeed. Through meditation and mindfulness, however, we allow ourselves to enter into a world of spiritual values and meaning, "olam ha-yetzirah"-the world of "formation", in which the separateness between ourselves and others starts to slip away and we begin to realize higher forms of life and deeper levels of perception and awareness. (The other two worlds of the spirit are "olam habriah"-the world of creation and "olam ha-atzilut", the world of "flowing", the highest spiritual rungs in which all is One and the line between the self of the individual and the Self of God no longer exists.)

So essential is the spiritual act of meditative mindfulness, that a martyr of the Warsaw Ghetto, a Hassidic rebbe, Rabbi Kalonymous Kalman Shapira, understood this practice to be central to the effort of any spiritual undertaking: "First, one simply watches for a set period of time, observing his thoughts. He eventually will notice that the mind is emptying; his thoughts are slowing a bit from their habitual flow. He then must repeat a single phrase, such as "God is truly God," in order to insert a thought of holiness into a now open mind. After these steps, he can then articulate a need for help in any one of the areas of character development, which he needs to work on, be it faith, love or awe.[113]

Sylvia Boorstein, a seminal thinker on the complementarities between Judaism and Buddhism, in her inimitably profound yet simple way has defined mindfulness as the disappearance of the personal ego into a universal space of sheer energy and serenity: "In periods of intensive meditation practice . . . I've seen the world I know and recognize as myself and my story dissolve and become the vibrancy of infinite space . . . . Things are just things . . . the place from which . . . the processes by means of which . . . the sentient, discriminating awareness of life begins, is revealed. It feels to me like the edge of creation . . . [114]

The Midrash makes this observation:" How many miracles does the Holy One, blessed be He perform for a man that he is not aware of? "[115] Not to be mindful or aware is a source of great misfortune and sadness; to "sleep" through life is an irretrievable loss. This unawareness brings to mind a passage in Alice Walker's The *Color Purple,* when one of her character records in her journal: "I've been so busy . . . . I never truly notice nothing God make. Not a blade of corn (how it do that?), not the color purple (Where it come from?). Not the little wild flowers. Nothing."[116]

The study of Torah, if undertaken with an eye toward spiritual enhancement, can get people "to surrender to the text, to engage with it in a playful and creative way, daring them to go in unexpected directions."[117]

Mindfulness touches on every aspect of the human experience, not only that which ostensibly is associated with the more abstract or spiritual. For example, the act of eating can become a powerful avenue to a greater awareness of life and its awesomeness, resulting in a deepening and on-going sense of gratefulness. Paying attention to the ordinary act of eating transforms this activity into one that is profoundly spiritual and meaningful. It is no accident that the Rabbis enjoined the following: "A man should taste nothing before he utters a blessing. Since "the earth is the Lord's, and all that it holds"[118], a man embezzles from God when he makes use of this world without a blessing." [119]

The Rabbis go even further in presenting to us the means by which eating is a mindful requirement, which expands our sense of gratefulness and wonder.

"Ben Zoma when seeing a large throng of people on the steps of the Temple Mount . . . said: Blessed be He who discerns secrets, and blessed be He who has created all those people to serve me. For he used to say: How many labors did Adam have to engage in before he obtained bread to eat! He plowed, he sowed he reaped; he stacked the sheaves, threshed the grain, winnowed the chaff, selected the good ears, ground them, sifted the flour, kneaded the dough and baked. And only then did he eat. Whereas I get up and find all these things done for me."[120] This ancient sage touched upon a spiritual phenomenon that is relevant to our contemporary lives. Our technological advances and the complexity of our lives, with their multitudes of divisions and fragmented areas of activity, have produced an ambience in which we are disconnected and alienated from the natural sources of our lives, which perhaps contributes greatly, to the difficulty in experiencing gratefulness. This act of eating, however, can be suffused with God's Presence and converted into an experience of authentic gratefulness and thanksgiving.

Aryeh Kaplan, the late, well-known interpreter of Kabbalah, in his *Jewish Meditation,* makes these insightful comments: "In Jewish teachings . . . it is taught that when a person eats, he should concentrate totally on the food and the experience of eating. Clearing the mind of all other thoughts, he should have in mind that the taste of the food is also an expression of the Divine in the food, that by eating it, he is incorporating the spark of the divine into his body. A person can also have in mind that he will dedicate the energy that he will obtain from this food to God's service. It is taught that when a person does this, it is counted as if the food he is eating is a sacrifice on the Great Altar in Jerusalem. Therefore, eating itself can be a form of meditation as well as a means to draw Closer to God." [121] We eat to socialize; to comfort ourselves when we are lonely, scared or depressed; or to keep stress or anger from getting out of control. If we eat gratefully, eating becomes a sacred and spiritually nurturing act.

One particular experience that made a deep impression on me while at the retreat program at Eilat Hayyim was the eating meditation. Each participant was given an item of food i.e., nuts, dried fruit, and instructed to eat not only slowly but mindfully. We first touched the food to gain a sense of its tactile texture; then we smelled the item to make conscious the olfactory aspect of the eating experience. When we had the food in our mouths, we did not chew and swallow quickly or immediately but rather let the food rest in our mouths to mindfully become aware of the foods' various qualities of solidity and taste, the subtle dimensions and sources of giftedness each food item could impart to us. Only at the end of this process were we instructed to swallow. Each meal thereafter became a marvelous experience in mindfulness eating which greatly enhanced the spiritual meaning of the act and imbued us further with the sense of greater gratefulness for our food.

At the conclusion of the retreat, I remember my first meal with my family. They were utterly astounded when they observed how I ate, slowly and with mindful deliberation. This was in stark contrast to how I used to gobble down my food and be the first to finish the meal at the family table. Food has become a source of great wonder and giftedness, a genuine mystery and reason for endless gratefulness and praise.

Mindfulness is an avenue by which we can arrive at an awareness of the ordinary as something "extraordinary." Regularity need not become rote-like and tedious. People usually consider walking on water or thin air a miracle. But I think the real miracle is not to walk either on water or in thin air, but to walk on earth. Every day we are engaged in a miracle which we don't recognize: a blue sky, white clouds, green leaves, the black, curious eyes of a child-our own two eyes. All is a miracle.

Maimonides, the thirteenth century Rabbi, philosopher and physician, in describing the essence of the love of God, saw that pondering the marvels of life led to gratefulness. He writes: "and what is the way that will lead to the love of Him and the fear of Him? When a person contemplates His great and wondrous works and creatures and through them obtains a glimpse of His wisdom which is incomparable and infinite, he will straightaway love Him, glorify Him and long with an exceeding longing to know His great name; and when he ponders these matters, he will recoil affrighted and realize that he is a small creature, lowly and obscure, endowed with slight and slender intelligence, standing in the presence of Him who is perfect in knowledge."[122] Maimonides understood that the way to God was the way of mindful gratefulness. This was the purpose of Torah.

Going Grateful

The human senses of hearing, sight, taste, touch and smell are all pathways to gratefulness. The first statement of the 'Shema'-Hear—highlights the capacity to listen as a divine gift and path to joy and delight.

Alone in a room with the lights off and your eyes closed, listen to your favorite piece of music. Let the music be the focus of your gratefulness meditation. Hear the beauty of the music with your grateful heart.

The third paragraph of the Shema singles out a simple blue thread as the focus of our sense of sight, visual awareness. The fringes, the 'Tzitzit,' are gazed upon as a stimulus to attentiveness. If you have a prayer shawl, a "talit," drape it around your shoulders and gaze upon the blue thread associating to the beauty and majesty of the blue seas and the blue sky. This may also lead you to think about God.

Visit an art museum and spend at least ten minutes in front of one piece of art. Look at it carefully; focus on it until you feel you are beginning to understand it, and to feel its message. Be grateful for your eyes that can see the beauty of line, color and texture. Recite quietly either or both of the following two statements.

I AM GRATEFUL FOR WHAT I SEE. BLESSED ARE YOU WHO OPENS THE EYES OF THOSE WHO CANNOT SEE.

Make use of your gratefulness journal in describing what you have heard and seen that enabled you to feel how gifted you are for having the ability to hear and see the things of beauty in this world.

Mindfully engage your sense of taste, smell and touch as you eat. Recite before eating:

WE PRAISE YOU FOR BRINGING FORTH BREAD FROM THE EARTH
WE PRAISE YOU WHO GRACIOUSLY SUSTAINS THE WORLD WITH KINDNESS PROVIDING ALL CREATURES WITH FOOD.

Before eating, look at the food, notice its colors and textures. Sit for a moment and simply smell its aromas. Take a small bite and experience the taste slowly on your palate, chewing deliberately to sense the texture of the food. The key to eating gratefully is to focus on the food without distraction and experience the richness of every morsel.

Consider the "food chain"—the farmer, the trucker, the food inspector, the wholesaler, the grocery store—and ultimately the Giver of all things, and remember those who are hungry. Rather than feeling guilty, feel grateful and from the place of gratitude, respond compassionately.

AVODAH—WORSHIP

It doesn't have to be
The blue iris, it could be
Weeds in a vacant lot, or a few
Small stones; just
Pay attention, then patch
A few words together, and don't try
To make them elaborate, this isn't a contest but the doorway
Into thanks, and a silence in which
Another voice may speak. [123]

—Mary Oliver

From Torah, the mindful awareness of life as a marvelous gift, we arrive at the second path bringing us closer to the world of gratefulness: "avodah," worship, the activity of the heart directed to the divine, the soulful awareness of God's compassion and generosity that engenders a response of gratefulness in the form of prayer.

However, the mechanization and formalization of prayer can become an irritant and a source of tremendous conflict and anger. The mere repetition of so many words can lead not only to boredom but also to a sense of futility and to spiritual and emotional blandness and isolation. Furthermore, instead of grasping prayer as an act of giving, often we are stuck on prayer as an attempt at "getting"!

From the need to develop spiritual mindfulness, an acute awareness of life's "allness" and uniqueness, the on-going challenge of Torah, the second gateway in our journey is grateful mindfulness. For the believer, grateful mindfulness *is* prayer. It was the late Louis Finkelstein, of blessed memory, rabbi, scholar and chancellor of the Jewish Theological Seminary for over three decades, who once differentiated the effort of studying the Torah from praying by saying the following:" When you study Torah, it is God talking to you; when you pray, you are talking to God."

To better understand the meaning and purpose of prayer, the words of another sage of a very different tradition are most apt. In *Peace is Every Step*, Thich Nhat Hanh raises a simple but very spiritually important question. "We often ask, "What's wrong?" Doing so, we invite painful seeds of sorrow to come up and manifest. We feel suffering, anger, and depression, and produce more such seeds. We would be much happier if we tried to stay in touch with the healthy, joyful seeds inside us and around us. We should learn to ask, 'What's not wrong?' and be in touch with that." [124] When we pray, not only are we talking to God, but in fact God is also talking to us, asking us two possible questions in the hope that we answer with the right question. He asks: "What's wrong?" and there is room in our prayer to voice our unhappiness, pain and suffering. At the same time, God asks: "What's not wrong?" When we pray as a response to what is not wrong in our lives and in the world, we embark on a journey of gratefulness which allows us to praise God, see the wonder of the world and the gift of our lives, and leave our prayers uplifted, thankful, and prepared to greet and embrace life with a renewed sense of compassion and love.

Robert Fulghum phrases this idea in very simple yet moving terms. "When small miracles occur for ordinary people, day by ordinary day; when not only did the worst not happen, but maybe nothing much happened at all, or some little piece fell neatly into place. The grace of what-might-have-been-but-wasn't, and it was good to get off scot-free for once. The ecstasy of what-could-never-happen but-did, and it was grand to beat the odds against for a change. Or the bliss of just what-was-for-a-day when nothing special took place-life just worked . . .

My grandfather says he blesses God each day when he takes himself off to bed having eaten and not having been eaten once again. "Now I lay me down to sleep. In the peace of amateurs, for whom so many blessings flow, I thank you, God, for what went right today! Amen." [125]

If you haven't got all the things you want, be grateful for the things you don't have that you don't want.

To be able to say "thank you" from the depths of one's being is a genuine prayer, for it touches the core of one's soul. Albert Einstein said: "If the only prayer you ever say in your life is thank you, it will be enough"

An important concept of Rabbinic Judaism is that of "Kavanah"—directed intention, deliberation or mindful awareness when performing a mitzvah, a sacred duty or obligation. Whether Kavanah is required or not for the proper discharge of the religious duty is the subject of extensive rabbinic discussion. When it comes to prayer, however, "avodah shebalev"-service of the heart—is a fundamental requirement.

Maimonides, for example, ruled that "prayer without "kavanah," intention, is not prayer" (Yad, Tefillah, 4:15) while the Code of Jewish Law states that "better a little supplication with "kavanah," than a lot without it." (Orach Hayim 1:4). Because prayer is an almost entirely internal act, the intentionality, the thought or feeling levels accompanying the recital of words, are vital to the prayerful experience. It should be noted that there are methods and techniques to prayer-prescribed words, ways by which they are to be formally articulated: softly or loudly, while standing or sitting, bowing or taking several steps forward or backward. Nonetheless, as "the service of the heart," it is essentially a subjective experience modified only by the sharing of words that are formalized as worship for an entire community, thus adding a dimension of objectivity to the enterprise.

Heschel, in a most penetrating way, points out that "Kavanah is more than paying attention to the literal meaning of the text. It is attentiveness to God . . . . an act of appreciation of being able to stand in the presence of God . . . Kavanah is insight, appreciation . . . an awareness of God rather than the awareness of the reason for a mitzvah (holy deed)." [126]

It is humanly impossible to gain the full measure of mindfulness or "Kavanah" at all times. However, even a moment of focus upon God and the ability to go beyond one's self-interest or concern is in fact a moment of profound mindfulness. Heschel continues: "When we analyze the consciousness of a supplicant, we discover that it is not concentrated upon his own interests, but on something beyond the self . . . Thus, in beseeching Him for bread, there is one instant, at least, in which your mind is directed neither to our hunger nor to food, but to His mercy. This instant is prayer."[127]

The meaning of prayer is poetically and movingly described by Wolf of Zhitomir, an 18th century Hassidic writer:

> "Do not think that the words of prayer as you say them go up to God:
> It is not the words themselves that ascend;
> It is rather the burning desire in your heart
> That rises like the smoke toward heaven.
> If your prayer consists only of words and letters and does not contain your
> heart's desire-
> How can it rise up to God?"[128]

When considering prayer, the second leg of the tripod upon which the spiritual world stands, prayer's essence is the praise of God.

> *Does God need our praise? I think not!*
> *'It is good to give thanks.' (Psalm 92)*
> *Why? Does God need our praise?*
> *No.*
> *We Do.*
> *To awaken wonder,*
> *To holiness*
> *To God.*
> *It is good to give thanks*
> *For through thanksgiving comes awakening*[129].
> —Rami M. Shapiro

Why engage in a constant, daily obligatory act of praising God? The repetitiveness of such praise can be very "off-putting" for both beginner and experienced "daavener" alike. What purpose does it serve?

When we praise, we recognize the "price", the "value" of the object being lauded. The Hebrew word for praise is Hallel. Interestingly, a cognate word of Hallel is "Yahel," meaning emitting light or luminescence. Thus, when we engage in prayer, we find a way by which to acknowledge the luminescence of the world, a reflection of God Himself, and in so doing, we articulate feelings of gratefulness. Prayer and gratitude go hand in hand. It is the Talmud's opinion that, "It is reasonable to regard service i.e. prayer, and thanksgiving as one."[130]

Several years ago, my family was sitting "Shiva", the week of mourning, in memory of my uncle. As we sat together, his son, a successful and well-respected physician who was the perennial skeptic in the family, asked why we praise God so much. "Does He really need our praises? Is His ego so fragile that He has to be reassured of His greatness?" My answer was, "No, He does not need our praises for His ego; we need to praise Him for our ego!" To praise is to rise above our limited selves. If we are to expand our sense of self to embrace more than the narrowness of our constricted individual lives, praising God as the object of a Reality beyond ourselves allows us the spiritual reach that transcends our grasp. Thus praise nurtures our identities as worthy human beings.

An everyday analogy: Why does a parent insist that her child say "thank you" when receiving a gift or favor? While it is pleasant and satisfying to be recognized by one's children, the expression of gratitude is more important for their character and spiritual education. The child's "thank you" is more necessary to the child than it is to the parent or adult.

A telltale sign of maturity is the independence of the individual, one's achieving emotional freedom from the need of approval at any cost. God is God precisely because of His unconditional and unqualified Oneness, independence and freedom. His identity is firmly rooted in His godliness and His "ego'" is utterly self-sufficient. As a matter of fact, Jewish tradition has recognized the most insightful of paradoxes. "In every passage where you find the greatness of God mentioned, there you will find also His humility".[131]

Knowing the need of man to praise, God overcomes, if you will, His discomfort with excessive praise and, in all humility, urges us to praise Him only so that we become increasingly aware of the gifts of life and incorporate a sense of gratefulness into our on-going experience.

David Steindl-Rost, a Benedictine monk, writes, "Even if we knew how the whole universe worked, we should still be surprised that there is a universe at all." [132]

The Hebrew poet, Hillel Zeitlin, understood the gift of creation this way:

> *Father of all worldly things:*
> *You create your world afresh*
> *Each passing second,*
> *And were you to withdraw*
> *Your loving kindness from creation*
> *All would be nothing in the twinkling of an eye.*
> *But moment-by-moment you empty*
> *The vessels of blessing*
> *Upon your creatures*

The morning stars appear again
And sing their love song;
And the sun sallies forth boldly
To sing its song of strength . . .

And the poor man cloaks himself again
And bares his heart to you:
And again his soul's prayer
Cleaves your heavens as it ascends before you,

And again his body breaks
Beneath your terrible glory;
And again his eye is lifted toward you.

But one ray of your light
And I abound in light;
But one word from you
And I am reborn,
But one tremor of your eternal life,
And I am drenched in the dew of childhood.

O you who create all anew,
O Father, create me, your child anew,
Breathe in me the breath of your nostrils
And I will live a new life,
Even a new life of childhood.[133]

Understood as an act of expressing gratefulness, prayer is not a means to an end, but an end in itself. The all-embracing nature of prayer was expressed by a contemporary American writer this way: "It was before we were called man or woman, even before we could speak one word. In those days we prayed with our entire beings; in the wind, in the sun, in the rain: every second, every day, every hour of our lives; at the rising of the sun and the dark of the moon, at the birth of the son and the death of a grandmother, at the wedding of two lovers, at the buzzing of spring. We breathed, we loved, we laughed, and we wept. This was before we call it prayer."[134] Penima V. Adelman

Several years before Abraham Joshua Heschel's death in 1972, he suffered a near fatal heart attack from which he never fully recovered. A disciple, (Rabbi Samuel Dresner) traveled to his apartment to see him. Rabbi Heschel spoke slowly and with some effort. "Sam," he said, "When I regained consciousness, my first feelings were not of despair or anger. I felt only gratitude to God for my life, for every moment I had lived. I was ready to depart. "Take me, O lord," I thought, "I have seen so many miracles in my lifetime." He added: "This is what I meant when I wrote (in the preface of his book of Yiddish poems):" "I did not ask for success; I asked for wonder. And You gave it to me." (Yiddish-Khob gebetn vunder anshtok glik, un du host zey mir gegebn)[135]

Going Grateful

As you sit and breathe calmly, with eyes closed, recite the following quietly:

> WE THANK YOU FOR THE MIRACLES THAT DAILY ATTEND US, FOR THE WONDERS AND GIFTS THAT ACCOMPANY US EVENING, MORNING AND NOON.

Continue your meditation by contemplating the everyday natural occurrences of life. Bring to your mind's eye a memory of a beautiful sunrise or sunset, a particularly striking appearance of the moon, the stars on a clear night, being in a garden surrounded by a cascade of color.

Repeat the following.

> THANK YOU FOR THE RISING AND SETTING OF THE SUN.
> THANK YOU FOR THE MOON AND STARS
> THANK YOU FOR COOL, REFRESHING RAIN.
> THANK YOU FOR THE ROSE AND THE CACTUS.

Before engaging in formal prayer, prepare yourself by meditating on the privilege to pray. Use a ritual object to enhance your feeling of relationship to the divine. Drape the talit, the prayer shawl over your head, sensing its protective quality, its enfolding your body like a canopy that will guard you against all danger. Feel the softness of the wool, the tent-like experience of feeling safe. Feel the straps of the tefillin, the phylacteries, how they bind you to a people, a history and a God—how grateful you can be for this connection.

Select five things that went wrong in the course of your morning activity. Record them in your gratefulness book or think about them. In the evening, consider five things that went right in the experience of that afternoon. Compare how you felt in the morning to your feelings in the afternoon.

GEMILLUT CHASSADIM—COMPASSION

When you look back on a lifetime
And think of what has been given to the world
By your presence . . .
Inevitably you think of your art . . . as the gift you have made
To the world in acknowledgment of the gift
You have been given, which is life itself . . .
That work is not an expression of the desire for praise or recognition,
  or prizes,
But the deepest manifestation
Of your gratitude for the gift of life. [136]

—Stanley Kunitz

The third indispensable fork in the road of grateful living is "Gemilut Chassadim", loving kindness and compassion. Gratefulness simultaneously feeds compassion as it is nurtured by it. It is this component of the spiritual life that is the tangible realization of the inner reality of gratefulness and the awareness of a Giving Source in the universe. The connection between prayer and acts of loving-kindness reverberates in the reality of "chessed'"—compassion, as the spiritual wellspring of life.

To pray is not to ask for things but to link ourselves to the essence of life that we understand to be "chessed", love, kindness and compassion. When we beseech God "to remember Your mercy" we are trying to do the same in our own lives, that is, to touch our own sense of compassion.

To pray is to see the world from the perspective of compassion. This awareness prompts compassionate action. The words "genius" and "generous" come from the same Latin root "genere", to generate, to "beget." The spiritual genius of living is being grateful in a way that begets generosity and compassion. The more you feel grateful, the greater is the impulse and inclination to give. Lewis Smedes, a professor of theology and ethics at Fuller Theological Seminary notes, "When I feel the joy of receiving my heart nudges me to join creation's ballet, the airy dance of giving and receiving, and getting and giving again." Receiving out of grateful awareness, from the vantage point of deep humility and gratitude, pries open the heart to respond with generosity and kindness. Doing acts of goodness is the natural outpouring of a grateful heart. These acts, in Heschel's words, "reflect the hidden light of His Holiness . . . it is within our power to mirror His unending love in deeds of kindness, like brooks that hold the sky."[137]

The quality of compassion is the essential and indispensable component of Godliness and as such every act of compassion is indeed a reflection of God's reality and Holiness. Towards the end of his life, Heschel said "When I was young, I used to admire people of intelligence; as I grow older, I admire people of kindness."

In my spiritual quest I have always battled the feeling of having to do something good because it was an obligation. Often, the motivation for goodness was the fear of punishment or misfortune. I yearned for another emotional way, another rationale that would be kinder and gentler than Thou shalt or Thou shalt not. Mindful prayer as the way to gratefulness was the approach that I began to arrive at by which to respond more kindly and compassionately to the world. I began to understand that fullness, a sense of being satisfied, finds its outlet in giving. As J. M. Coetzee, In *Age of Iron,* captures its essence when his heroine commenting on the reason she is inclined to feed a homeless person sleeping in an alley near her house asserts: "Why do I give this man food? For the same reason I would feed his dog if it came begging. For the same reason I gave you my breast. To be full enough to give and to give from one's fullness; what deeper urge is there?"

"Come into His presence with an offering."[138] The acclamation or praise of God is concretized through the bringing of a gift. As God gives all, we reciprocate when we give and when we share with others, and in this way reflect the godliness of the world.

"Gemilut hassadim," compassion and loving kindness, embraces a much wider context than mere giving. The Hebrew word—"Gomel"-entails a great deal more than surrendering ownership of something material and passing it on to someone else who may be in need. The word carries with it the implications of "bestowing upon," of entering into a relationship of compassion, love and service with others so that every response is defined by that commitment to compassion. Not only in tangible acts but in words and how we say them, in gestures and non-verbal communications of feelings and emotions, in levels of sincerity and openness, in desiring to be of service as a way of life: all of these components are contained in the spiritual state of being a "gomel" chessed.

One of the finest articulations of the religious meaning of "chessed" originates in the writings of Professor Isadore Twersky. In Tradition: A Journal of Orthodox Jewish Thought, he provides some invaluable insights into the nature of philanthropy, and more widely, of "chessed", as a uniquely core Jewish value-concept and "mitzvah" ... "Chessed" is that distinctive function which legitimizes our worldly existence and adds a new dimension of purposive ness to life ... God has abdicated part of a function of His in order to enable man to continue and extend creation.... Chessed is the most emphatic of God's attributes; the world came into existence because of chessed; the majority of God's actions toward man are characterized by chessed. The Torah begins and ends with loving-kindness as a divine act.[139] The practice of chessed thereby becomes man's "most God-like act," aiding the needy.... is comparable to aiding God Himself.... equating charity to the poor with a loan to God!" [140]

Jewish tradition emphasizes the religious imperative to walk in God's ways, to emulate God. "To walk in His Ways (Deut. 11:22). These are the ways of the Holy One—just as God is gracious and compassionate, you, too, must be gracious and compassionate. "The Lord is faithful in all His ways," as the Holy One is faithful, you too must be faithful. As the Holy One is loving, you too, must be loving."[141]

"As He clothes the naked, you should clothe the naked. The Holy One visited the sick, so should you visit the sick. The Holy One comforted the bereaved, so should you comfort those who are bereaved; The Holy One buried the dead; You should bury the dead."[142]

Thus compassion embraces the fullest experience and spiritual capacities and skills of the human mind and heart. Essentially, it becomes an integral part of one's life and fulfills the triangular configuration of Jewish spirituality.

A basic characteristic of "gemilut Chassadim", of service to others that enhances and deepens its authenticity and power, is that it represents its own reward.

Rabbi M. Shapiro put it simply when he said;

> *We are here to do*
> *and through doing to learn*
> *And through learning to know*
> *And through knowing to experience wonder*
> *And through wonder to attain wisdom;*
> *And through wisdom to find simplicity;*
> *And through simplicity to give attention;*
> *And through attention*
>
> *To see what needs to be done* ... [143]

Going Grateful

Take several deep breaths. Once settled into normal breathing, visualize your heart softening, receiving love from the universe, loved ones, even strangers.

As you exhale, let the love pass through you to those you already love, to those you hardly know, and to those with whom you are angry.

Begin to recite quietly to yourself the following phrases:

May I be filled with loving-kindness?
May I be grateful?
May I be peaceful,
May I feel blessed.

Repeat the phrases over and over again, letting the feelings fill your body and your mind.

When you feel ready, select someone who has been kind to you and recite the phrases on his/her behalf:

May he be filled with loving-kindness,
May she be grateful
May he be peaceful,
May she feel blessed.

Over time, you may include in your attention and focus loved ones, strangers, and the entire universe.

Record in your gratitude journal an act of goodness or compassion that you performed for someone else. How did it feel? Describe the sense of meaning it added to your life. Perform an act of grateful compassion—give a flower to a friend; send a card of caring to someone who is alone or ill; visit an elderly or infirmed person; share an encouraging word with a child; smile at a cashier, a gas attendant, someone waiting in line with you etc.

CHAPTER 12

FROM GRATEFULNESS TO LOVE

"Love is gratitude for being"
—Saul Bellow, *Humboldt's Gift,* P.392 (Viking Press, 1975)

"Love" is probably the most popular word on the planet. For love to be not only meaningful but also sustainable, it is necessary to understand it in terms of gratefulness. Without the core dimension of gratefulness, love becomes an experience of transience and impermanence. One cannot love without gratefulness nor can one be grateful without love.

Consider some of its definitions. The dictionary defines love as "including affection for reasons of kinship, sexual desire, admiration, and concern." For most, love connotes feeling, deep emotion that is tied to desire, attachment, liking and wishing to be with. In popular contemporary life, the notion of love is most prominent in its romantic and erotic associations.

When we say, "I love you," what do we mean, what do we feel? Is it a vague and diffused feeling of wanting to be with, to have, even to possess, the other? If so, then we fall short of the fullest capacity for love to be of greatest spiritual value in our lives.

To declare "I love you" is to assert our gratefulness for the one we love, to recognize the beloved as a gift to be taken care of, to be concerned about, to be cherished and for whom to feel thankfully joyful.

Martin Buber, a foremost Jewish theologian and thinker of the twentieth century, transposes the religious relationship between God and man to that which can prevail between one human being and another. "But I think that as we take, it is of the utmost importance to know that someone is giving.

One who takes what is given, and does not experience it as a gift, is not fully receiving; and so the gift turns into theft. But when we experience the giving, we find out that revelation exists."

Genuine love is synonymous with compassion. A church marquee conveyed this well: "One can give without loving, but you cannot love without giving." Love transcends sentiment or romantic emotion; love in the form of compassion is an approach to life and others, a relationship, and way of being with the fullness and totality of life. It is through love that God as Giver reaches the essence of divinity.

Bother David Steindl-Rast makes the following incisive observation: "We grow in love when we grow in gratefulness. And we grow in gratefulness when we grow in love. Here is the link between the two: thanksgiving pivots on our willingness to go beyond our independence and to accept the give-and-take between giver and thanks giver. But the "yes", which acknowledges our interdependence, is the very "yes" to belonging, the "yes" of love."[144]

In the Torah, while emotional components are very much part of the mosaic of love, emphasis is placed on the behavioral and relational dimensions of love. Most commentators interpret the "commandment" to love to suggest conduct and tangible concern rather than feeling, on the assumption that emotion cannot be legislated. In all the references to "genuine" love, the thrust of rabbinical interpretation is legal and ethical.

The most salient of Biblical statements about love is: "Love your neighbor as yourself."[145] This verse has become the foundation of most moral and ethical standards of human behavior. What does it mean? Can we love someone else as equally as we love ourselves? By nature, self-interest and survival are primary "instincts" or inherent components in the human psyche. If that is the case, how do we reach the point of equating love of others with love of ourselves?

Consider the commentary of the *Etz Chayim Torah*: "Love your neighbor because he or she is like yourself, subject to the same temptations as you are . . . . we should be prepared to judge the behavior of others charitably . . . because all human beings are part of the same body, to hurt another person . . . is to hurt part of oneself."[146]

Integral to loving is the awareness of unity that underlies all of human life. Love and the unity that pervades the universe are linked organically one to the other. The "Shema"-Judaism's central statement of faith—declares God as—"Echad"-"One" and "Unique." This declaration is preceded and followed by an avowal of "Love" as the unfolding of God's Presence to the Jewish people in the form of the gift of Torah and the accompanying expectation of Israel's reciprocal response of love toward God the Giver of Torah. But how does one love God? We know how to love humans, but in what way can we feel and demonstrate our love for an ephemeral, abstract, divine reality?

One traditional Jewish way is to maintain loyalty by observing God's Torah. If we are told that the performance if goodness, kindness and justice are the desires of God, then it follows naturally that love of God is realized through our actions of compassion and fairness.

A more universal approach to loving God is arrived at by loving the world. If we assume that the world was created by God, is it not logical to conclude that when we love the world i.e. feel grateful and responsible for all aspects of life, we fulfill the most sacred and special of all spiritual acts?

Every letter of the twenty-two letter Hebrew alphabet contains a numerical value from "aleph," the first letter that is equivalent to one until the last letter, "tav," four hundred. Jewish tradition makes use of these numerical values in its efforts to interpret sacred texts in a philosophically and spiritually meaningful manner. This exegetical approach is called, "gematria."

A tantalizing "gematria reinforces the intimate intertwining of unity and love as manifestations of the Divine. "Echad"-One or Unique—has the numerical equivalence of thirteen. "Ahavah"-Love-likewise contains the sum of thirteen. Together, they add up to twenty-six, the numerical value of the "tetragrammaton"—the original name of God—"Yud Heh Vav Heh." (Yud=10; Heh=5; Vav=6; Heh=5) God becomes concretized whenever and wherever love and unity find expression and realization in the context of human life.

Gratefulness opens our hearts to embrace the world with love. Love is the link to Oneness and from that unity love flows like a stream of refreshing water that touches every tributary of dryness and despair. As each human being recognizes that we are all an inseparable part of this unity, the desires and the cravings of the individual as individual recede and fall away so that the soul can receive the Oneness of all things that bind us together like the knots of the "Talit"—the prayer shawl and those of the phylacteries, the "tefilin."

What enhances one's capacity to be grateful is the awareness that we are all interconnected into a unity of being and purpose. Moreover, "echad" also suggests "singularity" both of God and man, and thus deepens our sense of self-value and regard for all others and ourselves. We emerge, therefore, grateful for this gift of uniqueness that is shared by all. The recognition of the bipolar spiritual dimension of unity and uniqueness unfolds and articulates itself in love of oneself, of others, and the Source of this gift. Thus, the "Shema" with its insistence on Unity and Uniqueness, is bracketed by the love expressed in the prayer immediately preceding the "Shema", and the enjoining of the paragraph following the "Shema" to "Love the Lord your God with all your heart, with all your soul and with all your might."

Heschel links up the notion of God's unity with the mystery of the universe and the kinship shared by all human beings. "The intuition of that all-pervading unity has often inspired man with a sense of living in cosmic brotherhood with all beings ... We are all-men, stars, flowers, birds—assigned to the same cast, rehearsing for the same inexplicable drama. We all have a mystery in common-the mystery of being."[147]

As we open our hearts, we come to experience interconnectedness, the realization that all things are joined together and conditioned in an interdependent arising. Each experience and event contains all others.

The teacher depends on the student; the airplane depends on the sky.

When a bell rings, is it the bell we hear, the air, the sound at our ears, or is it our brain that rings? It is all of these things. The sound of the bell is here to be heard everywhere in the eyes of every person we meet, in every tree and insect, in every breath we take.

Holding up a piece of paper, Zen master Thich Nhat Hanh expresses it this way:

"If you are a poet, you will see clearly that there is a cloud floating in this sheet of paper. Without a cloud there will be no water; without water the trees cannot grow; and without trees, you cannot make paper. So the cloud is in here ... Let us think of other things, like sunshine. Sunshine is very important because the forest cannot grow without sunshine, and we as humans cannot grow without sunshine. So the logger needs sunshine in order to cut the tree, and the tree needs sunshine in order to be a tree. Therefore, you can see sunshine in this sheet of paper. And if you look more deeply ... you see not only the cloud and the sunshine in it, but that everything is here, the wheat that became the bread for the logger to eat, the logger's father—everything is in this sheet of paper ....

The presence of this tiny sheet of paper proves the presence of the whole cosmos.

When we truly sense this interconnectedness and the emptiness out of which all beings arise, we find liberation and a spacious joy."[148]

For those of a religious orientation, the love of God is the highest of all challenges: "You shall love the Lord Thy God, with all thy heart, with all thy soul and with all thy might." [149] Again: How do we love God? Listen to the traditional commentators. "Israel's duty to love God is inseparable from action and is regularly connected with the observance of His commandments . . . The command to love God may be understood as requiring one to act loyally toward Him, though an emotional response is also called for."[150]

Other contexts of love in the Torah expand the orbit of human concern. "The stranger who resides with you shall be to you as one of your citizens; you shall love him as yourself, for you were strangers in the land of Egypt."[151] An additional reference to "loving" the Egyptian is found in Deuteronomy 23:8 where it is written: "You shall not abhor an Egyptian for you were a stranger in his land." Traditional commentators offer two basic explanations for this injunction not to abhor, moreover, to love, the Egyptian. One, having been oppressed in the land of the Egyptians, we "might wish to be like them when we have the opportunity, oppressing the powerless in our midst. Therefore, the Torah warns us to use the memory of slavery in Egypt to learn empathy for the oppressed." [152] Two, "despite their enslavement of the Israelites, the Egyptians had provided a haven in a time of famine, for which Israel was to recognize a continuing debt of *gratitude*." [153]

In the latter opinion is the nub of the entire principle of spiritual love, the dynamic that bridges the emotional with the behavioral, the feeling with the act, and spiritually infuses the soul with the ability to rise above the natural inclination to hold a grudge, to hate and to seek vengeance or retaliation. The Bible presents us with a radically all-inclusive approach to ethical behavior toward others. We are enjoined to love not only those of our own family and clan, but the entire human community, even and especially our past enemies.

The outlook of gratefulness gives us the powerful capacity to discover a means of arriving at forgiveness and transforming an experience of great, even unspeakable agony and anguish, into a path of greater humanity, compassion and love. Without this special spiritual strength, we are prone to responses that can only add further shadows to the already existing darkness in our lives. It goes without saying, that this spiritual task is perhaps the most difficult and demanding of all. Yet, it is the only spiritually meaningful option available to us.

Yet, we are often reminded by science and the culture of today that the human being is selfish and constricted in a way that he or she is naturally and inescapably conditioned to act in ways that lead to hurt and the mistreatment of others. We are told that genetics determine our behavior, which often is so cruel and harmful. Only recently, the New York Times carried an article in its Science section entitled: "Payback Time: Why Revenge Tastes So Sweet", in which some research psychologists inform us that revenge is not some disease or moral failing or crime but "is primed in the genes . . . a deeply human and sometimes very functional behavior; . . . it can be a very good deterrent to bad behavior and bring feelings of completeness and fulfillment." [154] Nevertheless, religion's unique role in human development and the spiritual understanding of life is to inspire us to rise above biology and genetics and become more like the "angels" in our attempt to fulfill our natures as gifts of the divine Giver. And gratefulness is the way.

Going Grateful

An ancient Jewish legend tells of the 36 anonymous righteous individuals who support our spiritual universe. They could be anyone; they are recognized by their uninterrupted and indiscriminate acts of kindness and compassion. Think about ways you can emulate these spiritual heroes. Think of one person you deem to be particularly good and kind. Consider his/her acts of goodness. Write down a description of this person. Examine your feelings of gratefulness for knowing this person.

Think about a time when someone rendered you a kindness for no apparent reason, or forgave you for some error. How did you feel? Were you grateful? Write about the incident.

Recite: BLESSED ARE YOU WHO PROVIDES US WITH RIGHTEOUS AND COMPASSIONATE HUMAN BEINGS.

Recite: I AM THANKFUL FOR THE GOOD PEOPLE IN MY LIFE
I AM THANKFUL FOR THE GOOD PEOPLE OF THE WORLD
I AM THANKFUL FOR THE GIFT OF GOODNESS.

CHAPTER 13

GRATEFULNESS AND THE FAMILY: THE FAMILY GRATEFUL TOGETHER, STAYS TOGETHER

    In family relations, gratefulness is an essential ingredient for the emotional and spiritual well being of all its members. Interestingly, the Bible does not speak of loving one's children. The assumption is that paternal love does not need to be legislated. Implicitly, the love of children could be regarded as an outgrowth of one's sense of gratefulness for the gift of children.

    In the Biblical framework, offspring was indispensable to not only the survival of the family but to the continuity of the tribe and the people of Israel. From the inception of the Biblical narrative, blessing was intimately and inseparably attached to having children. "God blessed them and said to them: Be fertile and increase . . ."[155] Moreover, the barrenness of women was viewed as a terrible curse and a source of devastating sorrow for the women of the Bible. The matriarchs—Sarah, Rebecca and Rachel were all infertile until God eventually removed their barrenness and blessed them with children, thus highlighting the giftedness of children as a supreme blessing from God.

    In rearing and relating to our children which, by and large, is no easy task, (the Rabbis refer to it as—"Tzaar gidul Banim"—the pain of raising children), we know from research and everyday experience, that the absence of love can lead to disastrous results of stunted emotional growth, deep pain and rage, and anti-social behavior. Therefore, it is both psychologically and spiritually necessary to communicate one basic emotional message to our children—"I am grateful for your being my child."

The Besht, the Baal Shem Tov, founder of the Hassidic movement, was once approached by a father who complained that his son had forsaken God. "What, Rabbi, should I do?" "Love him more than ever," was the reply.

When parents convey their disappointment in their children, focusing primarily on the child's "imperfection" or indulging in the very destructive "comparison syndrome" by pointing to another child as the model of success, it is a sure fire recipe for anger, sadness, failure and estrangement. While it is natural to feel disappointment, even resentment at a child's "failure", it is precisely at these difficult moments that we call upon our awareness of life's fullness and blessing, cultivated over time, to allow our love and gratefulness to rise to the surface and be transmitted to our young.

While I was teaching senior high school students in a private parochial school, one student came to class unprepared for a test. He was an excellent student and when asked for an explanation he answered: "I couldn't study—I was up all night and very upset." I asked for the reason. His reply was: "I wasn't accepted to the University of Pennsylvania, early admission, and my father was very angry at me and bawled me out the whole night." His father was a graduate of that school and felt disappointed to the degree that he was unable to show his son the value of his gratefulness and love, especially when the boy needed it most.

I think of the countless Bar/Bat Mitzvah ceremonies during which sacredness degenerates into displays of status and success. It has not been infrequent when I have noticed, to my great chagrin, a grimace of anger and disappointment cross over the face of a parent in the event of the slightest error in the presentation of the Haftarah, the Biblical passage recited by the young Jewish adult, and the ensuing emotional devastation of the youngster.

As Rabbi Harold Kushner has so pointedly indicated in his writings and oral communications, children have become "Nachas machines", avenues of pride for parents rather than individual human beings in their own right for whom to be grateful. Psychologists describe this phenomenon as "achievement by proxy syndrome". Parents depend on their children's accomplishments for their own sense of identity, personal self-enhancement or unfulfilled dreams.

From the perspective of gratefulness, "good enough" is not an admission of failure or defeat. Rather, it is the recognition of what has been referred to as "ordinary holiness", the ability to acknowledge the holiness in all things because they were all created by God, the ultimate Giver. Gratefulness is the necessary emotional environment in which our young will realize their inherited potential.

Perhaps the greatest gift we can pass on to our children is the spiritual practice of gratefulness, which in fact, is a way of teaching our children how to love.

It is not uncommon for parents who are neither formally religious nor tradition oriented to have their children recite the "Shema"-the Hear O Israel prayer, before retiring. Perhaps, given the Shema's universal acceptance among most Jews, it is a simple, sparse and undemanding way by which to inculcate a sense of Jewish identification in their young. I would suggest that the more compelling reason for this practice is one of fear, one that has to do with the supposed dangers that stalk us during our sleeping hours. For whatever psychological reasons that may have be related to superstitious beliefs or those which originate from earlier times when the night hours were indeed perilous, we consider our children particularly vulnerable while they sleep. It is therefore no surprise that well meaning and sophisticated parents would want some level of divine protection for their kids. Personally I have no objection to this practice. As a matter of fact Jewish law mandates the "Kriat Shema Al Hamitah"—reciting these words together with others before one beds down for the night. There is little question in my mind that one of the over arching reasons is the psychological need for security at that time. Not infrequently do I personally make use of these prayers for purposes of garnering the sense of calm and security that will aid in my falling asleep.

While the value of saying the Shema at night is obvious, I would strongly recommend that children recite a different prayer each morning when they rise, a prayer referred to earlier as a foundation for gratefulness awareness for the entire day. "Modeh Ani Lefanecha"-I am grateful to You O Lord for restoring my soul, my life this morning. Not fear or petition but rather a sense of gratefulness and praise is the spiritual rationale and impetus for these words which are uttered literally at the crack of our consciousness. To educate our children to greet each day with gratefulness is a powerful instrument for character and moral education. Repeatedly and lovingly, the parent can create a climate of caring gratefulness each morning so that instead of the typical announcements of "I'm tired, I don't want to get out of bed, I want to stay in bed longer" which usually reflect a feeling of fear and wanting to regress into the safety of sleep, over time the young person and the adult will eventually incorporate gratefulness into the repertory of his psychological responses to meeting each day with greater hopefulness, eagerness and joy.

The most popular personal celebration in modern society is the birthday. In many earlier cultures, the birthday as an occasion to celebrate was entirely unknown. As a matter of fact, most people maintained only the vaguest sense of the date of birth of family or friends. In the Jewish world, for example, the date of one's birth was always associated with the time of public Jewish festival celebrations. If asked when one was born, the reply often was: "A week before Passover" or "three days after Purim." Furthermore, no one celebrated a birthday. Today by contrast, if a lavish birthday party is not held, this omission is construed as an act bordering on child abuse. Personally, I love birthdays. However, in the spirit of gratefulness and love I would suggest that the birthday be celebrated a little differently. When the child is old enough, it is my recommendation that not the son or daughter receive gifts and attention, but the parents. After all, without the parents the child would not have received the greatest of all gifts, the gift of life. Would it not be more fitting and spiritually enlightening for the one whose birth is being recognized to express gratefulness not by receiving gifts but by giving them to the source of their life?

We were chatting after Sabbath services. Standing alongside a table covered with soda bottles, his seven-year-old son was trying to pour himself some soda from a large bulky bottle into a tiny plastic cup. As to be expected, he spilled the soda on the table. His father then patiently showed him how to hold both the bottle and the cup so as not to repeat the accident. The boy appeared reassured and with confidence proceeded to pour his own cup of soda.

"What a patient parent you are," I commented.

"I try to teach my son to be self-sufficient, how not to complain but to try and overcome the difficulty. It's important for him to do this. He's been in remission for three and a half years."

I was at a loss for words. Cancer? At Three years of age? The boy was a mere child. Noticing my awkward discomfort he quickly added:" He's fine now. They removed the kidney with cancer and he's as good as new. He's a little insecure now, of course, but he'll get over that."

From what I could gather from his short time in the synagogue,
he was a most adorable, active and intelligent young boy.

"I want him to be able to cope with life and enjoy it. I tell him again and again: 'Don't say ouch; say wow!'"

Instead of ouch, say wow! What a wonderful lesson in teaching gratefulness.

The Torah does not legislate love of a child for a parent. It does, however, mandate "honor." The fifth of the Ten Commandments declares: "Kabed et avicha v'et eemehcha", "Honor your father and your mother." What does "honor" mean? The Rabbinic tradition enumerates a whole series of activities that the child is expected to fulfill in relating to his or her responsibilities to the parent. [156]

If we examine the term—"Kabed"—honor—we discover that it is derived from the same root as another word used in reference to God's immanence or glory, "Kavod." When we are directed to "honor" our parents, we are expected to relate to our parents in the same way we relate to God: with gratefulness in recognition of the gift of life.

Our Sages have taught: "There are three partners in a man: the Holy One, his father and his mother. When a man honors (demonstrates gratefulness to) his mother and father, the Holy One says: I account it to them as though I were dwelling among them, and they were honoring Me, read, being grateful to Me." [157]

Gratefulness is also a powerful and sustaining spiritual ingredient in the success and enrichment of a marital relationship. Unrealistic expectations arising out of life's changes may lead to serious disruptions in long standing marriages. The husband seeks out a younger woman to revitalize his "romantic life" and thereby gain a sense of renewed youthfulness. Because of a possible growing alienation of affections, the wife may search for emotional sustenance outside of the marriage. Here too the "comparison syndrome" contributes to and exacerbates the difficulties of the relationship. The husband may think: "She is not as pretty, sexy, smart or sensitive as, etc" or the wife may muse: "He's not as handsome, generous, manly or attentive as, etc." If one spouse articulates or emotionally communicates the ungratefulness embedded in this "comparison syndrome", what results are feelings of rejection, of being emotionally divorced and abandoned.

These feelings are often the product of one's own inability to be grateful for one's self, and thus the need to project the reason for dissatisfaction on others. An unreasonable desire for "perfection" in one's partner can be a source of great difficulty leading to an inability to appreciate the marriage for what it is.

A Sufi tale related the following: "One afternoon, Nasruddin and his friend were sitting in a café, drinking tea, and talking about life and love. "How come you never got married, Nasruddin?" asked his friend at one point. "Well," said Nasruddin, "to tell the truth, I spent my youth looking for the perfect woman. In Cairo, I met a beautiful and intelligent woman, with eyes like dark olives, but she was unkind. Then in Baghdad, I met a woman who was a wonderful and generous soul, but we had no interests in common. One woman after another would seem just right, but there would always be something missing. Then one day, I met her. She was beautiful, intelligent, generous and kind. We had everything in common. In fact, she was perfect." "Well," said Nasruddin's friend, "what happened? Why didn't you marry her?" Nasruddin sipped his tea reflectively, "Well," he replied, "it's a sad thing. Seems she was looking for the perfect man." [158]

This search for "perfection" leads to inevitable disappointment, eventually resulting in an emotional emptiness making a marriage relationship untenable. A marriage that has the seeds of flowering into a thing of beauty needs the nurturing of gratefulness to grow and blossom.

Kay Holler relates a daily ritual that her husband, Steve, initiated in their home, a ritual which seems small but is large with significance. "Every evening since we've been married, Steve comes home from work and shouts from the front door, "The luckiest man in the world is home!" I've been hearing this for two and half years now," writes Kay, "and it still makes me feel good."[159]

Going Grateful

When alone with spouse, friend or family, at a dinner table or simply sitting together in the living room, hold hands with your loved ones and companions and say to them: "I am grateful that you are my wife, husband, friend, son, daughter etc.-I love you." Speak further about how grateful you feel or sit quietly with loved ones and simply think about why you are grateful to have each other.

Write a letter to your spouse, companion, family member or child expressing how grateful you are to have them in your life. Have your child draw a picture of which they are grateful for in the family.

Before going to sleep, share with your spouse, companion or child one to three things for which you are grateful to them as a result of that day's experience. Before putting your children to bed, spend a moment or two asking them if they can think of one thing that they are particularly grateful for that they themselves did during the day and one thing that someone else did for them. If they are unable to do this, remind them of all the possibilities for gratefulness in their lives—a good book or story they read, friends, caring teachers, a delicious food they ate, something they learned that was new to them etc.

CHAPTER 14

GOD AND GRATEFULNESS

At the very center of the unfolding drama of life and the response of gratefulness is some consciousness of a God or a God idea. While metaphysical considerations connected to our understanding of God are of philosophical and intellectual importance, for me the psychological and spiritual dimensions are of greater meaning and personal significance.

The story is told of a kindergarten student who posed a theological question to his teacher for which she had no satisfying answer. The teacher hurried to the principal's office and invited her into the classroom to deal with this child's question. The child asked:" My teacher told me that God is everywhere. Well, I don't want a God who is everywhere; I want a God who is somewhere!"

The intuitive understanding of God's immanence, of finding a God not only beyond, but also within our lives, is to me the greatest of all spiritual challenges.

The conventional understanding of God is connected to four fundamental characteristics that constitute God's godliness, infinity, omnipotence, omniscience and benevolence. To gain a glimpse of God's reality, God's benevolence is the over arching spiritual principle of the universe while the other three attributes—infinity, omnipotence and omniscience—must be understood only in the service of the fourth, benevolence. What is often a source of immeasurable danger, even destruction and violence, is the priority that is assigned to God as omnipotent, with power being the quality that wins public allegiance often leading to an abuse of religion in human affairs. Sadly, this imbalance often fuels the flames of fundamentalism and violence. My assertion of seeing God as essentially a Giver of all things highlights God's benevolence and perforce brings us to an awareness of both humility and gratefulness as sources of nurturance and the enhancement of life.

While we cannot escape the portrayal of God as omnipotent emerging from the pages of Scripture and other ancient writings, we must, if religion is to serve the welfare of humanity, reach out to a God who is at the core, compassionate and giving.

The Psalmist declares poetically: "Praise Him, all you shining stars, the sun, the moon, you highest heavens . . . you waters above the heavens . . . all who share the earth, monsters of the seas and all its depths, fire and hail, snow and mist, storms . . . all you high mountains and hills, you fruit-bearing trees and cedars, all you wild beasts and cattle, you creeping creatures and birds . . . . the kings and all the people of the world . . . . men and women, young and old . . ."(Psalm 148).

At first glance, this statement appears to be mere metaphor, anthropomorphizing the world of nature in the act of praising God. I suggest that this verse and many other similar verses could be re-interpreted to mean something more spiritually penetrating than an ordinary, however beautiful, literary device. By investing the universe with the capacity to praise, the poet informs us that the world in its totality is suffused with a pervasive principle of gratefulness as an intrinsic dimension of spiritual reality. When one is grateful, he taps into the all-embracing reservoir of praise and gratefulness that lies at the heart of the world. This connection can provide the human being with a sense of peace and harmony, of Oneness, with all of life.

How do we find a God who is" somewhere", identifiable, meaningful, a source of immediacy and genuine closeness, which prompts us to do good, love mercy and act humbly? Where do we find a God whose very transcendence suggests His inaccessibility while at the same time demands our connection and relationship? Wherein lies the human dimension of this transcendence? Where is the meeting point between God and man?

The divine-mortal nexus is experienced through the dynamic of giving and receiving. God as Giver expects man as receiver to likewise give and in that way God becomes the recipient of His handiworks' acts of giving and generosity. A reciprocal partnership is entered into, a covenant crafted from ever unfolding threads of gratefulness and giving. The spiritual capacities of thanking, being grateful and recognizing God as Giver, witnessing the wonder in life, and valuing concern and compassion as the links of intersection between God and man, are the "transcendental" qualities in the human character that open the path to encountering the "transcendental ness" of

God and transforming that transcendence into an immediate and intimate immanence, changing the beyond to the being here.

Heschel, the super naturalist and existentialist, informs us that inherent in the very nature and heart of the spiritual universe is the reality of God: "Mystery is not an exception but an air that lies about all being, a spiritual setting of reality; not something apart but a dimension of all existence . . . there is holiness that hovers over all things . . . The natural and the supernatural are not two different spheres, detached from one another as heaven and earth. God is not beyond but right here; not only close to my thoughts but also to my body . . . . In His otherness, ineffable and immediate as the air we breathe and do not see, which enables us to see His distant nearness."[160]

Another major Jewish thinker, Mordechai M. Kaplan, founder of the Reconstructionist movement that rejects the notion of a supernatural God, sees divinity as part of the natural world, yet distinctly apart from it. "There is only one universe within which both man and God exist. The so-called laws of nature represent the manner of God's immanent functioning. The element of creativity, which is not accounted for by the so-called laws of nature, and which points to the organic character of the universe or its life as a whole, gives us a clue to God's transcendent functioning . . . God is the life of the universe, immanent insofar as each part acts upon every other, and transcendent insofar as the whole acts upon each part."[161]

In tangible terms that touch our lives, Heschel's metaphysical understanding of God as the source of everlasting and spiritual concern for man is not far removed from Kaplan's sociological and pragmatic awareness of God's attributes of spiritual and ethical meaning in human life. Both perspectives allow us to assert the worthwhile ness and significance of life as the foundation of the human condition, which in Kaplan's phrasing, is a contemporary interpretation of the concept of "holiness."[162] Both come to a conclusion that God's immanence is God's concern, love, and passion for justice that signify the wellspring of the spiritual and moral aspirations of the Jewish people and all people everywhere.

In his diary, Mordechai M. Kaplan, makes an important entry on June 22, 1930, in which he stresses the centrality of gratitude as *the* basic religious virtue and suggests ways by which gratefulness can and must be taught to the young. "It is as impossible for a person who is devoid of a native sense of gratitude to have religious experience as it is for the tone deaf to appreciate music. It is the capacity for thankfulness which enables a person to discern elements of worth while ness and significance in life . . . . religion is essentially the experience of the worth while ness and significance of reality as a whole to the individual human being and of the group to which one belongs . . . . Worship will have but one function, that of imbuing us with God consciousness, or the consciousness of life's worth while ness . . . . It will therefore express itself in words and gestures of "tehillah" rather than "tefillah", of praise rather than petition." [163]

Traditionalism on the one hand and Reconstructionism on the other share the very same fundamental idea and quest of religion, namely the cultivation of gratefulness as the essential foundation of religion's spiritual structure. Perhaps the capacity for gratefulness can be viewed as the point of convergence not only between Heschel and Kaplan, but in fact, among people of any and all religious orientations. Beyond a particular and formal religious pattern of thought and behavior, a common denominator of human spirituality is the component of gratefulness as the bedrock of universal moral behavior and a sense of unity in the world.

The Rabbis tell us: "Hakol b'yedei shamayim chutz meyirat shamayim"— "Everything is in the hands of Heaven, except the "fear"—the awe of Heaven." A remarkable moral gift given to the human being is the freedom to choose to live in such a way that one's life reflects the "awe of heaven", that is the awareness of life as a source of wonder and amazement.

God as Giver of all things is unable to do one thing; He cannot determine gratefulness. He gives everything, but like one who gives a gift, cannot be certain whether the receiver will be grateful or not. God as Giver is, if you will, constrained in this one area of gratefulness. No matter how narrow or expansive the gift, whether it is received with an open and grateful heart or whether it is repudiated out of disappointment and hardness of heart, the choice is the ultimate mark of one's essential humanity. "Behold, I have put before you life and death, blessing and curse . . . choose life."[164] The choice to be grateful is a choice of greater humanity, blessing and life.

The Talmud tells us: "Rabbi Judah said in the name of Rab: There are four classes of people who need to offer thanksgiving; Those who have crossed the sea, those who have traversed the wilderness, one who has recovered from an illness and a prisoner who has been set free."[165] Notice that unlike other religious practices, the inclination of giving thanks for being delivered is not a formal obligation. The Talmud does not use the word-"Hayyavim"-obliged; instead they express the thanksgiving requirement as one embedded in one's spiritual and psychological need-"Tzrichin"-need to thank. The Talmud understood that the experience of gratefulness is inherent in the human soul and it is one's choice to articulate this sense through words of blessing. By so doing, we rise to a place of spiritual advancement and wholeness.

Gratefulness is a significant principle by which we can organize and interpret the world for the benefit of all. There is an underlying need for people to see the world as an orderly place, a place of some predictability, with a trust and faith that life is essentially worthwhile and that a better future awaits our children and us. The cultivation of gratefulness opens our hearts to this sense of trust. At the core of this perception is the reality that we have been given to by an Ultimate Giver, and in recognizing this Source of reliability and dependability, we remain confident that the gift of life and all its myriad blessings will go on.

Whether God is understood as a Power that makes for salvation, seeing religion from a functional point of view, that which is socially determined and necessary (Kaplan), or a Personality that is intimately related to humanity and "needs "man for His fulfillment and for the redemption of the world (Heschel), a sense of wonder wedded to gratefulness and the ability to give thanks is the cornerstone of human spiritual existence. Kaplan and Heschel share one fundamental conviction, the worthwhile ness and wonder of life.

It has been said: Life is a gift; our job is to learn to receive it. At the end of the day, the God who is "Somewhere" is the God who is "Everywhere." The "allness" of life points to God. It is this "everywhere" or "allness" that inspires us to say" thank you" to the God who is "Somewhere" as Giver of everything.

CHAPTER 15

SOME PERSONAL AFTERTHOUGHTS

While we witness pain and sorrow, the path to inner joy is one that is paved by the heart's awareness of the reality of compassion and goodness that inhere in the totality of life. Perhaps this awareness is the first small step in our journey not to the moon, but to that reality that bestows upon all of us the marvel and wonder of the moon and of all creation.

THE GOOD NEWS

The good news
They do not print.
The good news
We do print.
We have a special edition every moment,
And we need you to read it.
The good news is that you are alive,
And the linden tree is still there
Standing firm in the harsh winter
The good news is that you have wonderful eyes
To touch the blue sky.
The good news is that your child is there before you,
And your arms are available:
Hugging is possible.
They only print what is wrong.
Look at each of our special editions.

> *We always offer the things that are not wrong,*
> *We want you to benefit from them*
> *And help protect them.*
> *The dandelion,*
> *Is there by the sidewalk,*
> *Smiling its wondrous smile*
> *Singing the song of eternity.*
> *Listen! You have ears that can hear it.*
> *Bow your head.*
> *Listen to it.*
> *Leave behind the world of sorrow*
> *And preoccupation*
> *And get free.*
> *The latest good news*
> *Is that you can.*[166]
> —Thich Nhat Hanh

As I stood at the starting line surrounded by a sea of eager and excited runners, the sun was warm and bright, inching its way across the crystal-clear sky pointing to the prospect of weather which is not ideal for a marathon of 26.2 miles.

The Verrazano Bridge beckoned us toward the unknown horizon. I recited: "Praised are You, Lord our God, Sovereign of the Universe, who has kept us alive, sustained us and enabled us to reach this day." I then stepped into the future.

Five hours and fifty minutes later, I crossed the finish line in Central Park, having wound my way, along with 37,000 others, through the never-ending streets that is New York City, the mantra of "MODEH"—"I THANK" and "EYEH"—"I WILL BE," on my lips. I was grateful to God, to the open heart of New York City, to family and friends for their support, and at the age of 65 years and one week, I ran the full 26.2-mile distance of the NYC marathon.

My final words were: "Praised are You . . . who is good and who bestows the good on all things."

> *Thanks for all you made,*
> *Thanks for all you gave me*
> *Insight and understanding*
> *A friend or two,*

For all that I have in the world:
A flowing song
And a forgiving heart-
Because of all this, I go on.

Thanks for all you made,
Thanks for all you gave me-
A child's laughter,
Blue skies,
A piece of land and a warm home;
A place to sit,
Loving friends-
Because of all this, I go on.

Thanks for all you made,
Thanks for all you gave me-
A day of happiness,
Honesty and integrity,
A sad day that is gone:
The victory of two thousand years
And the white wings of peace-
Because of all this, I go on.[167]
—Uzi Hitman

CHAPTER 16

MORE GRATEFULNESS MEDITATIONS

"Ven me zol Got danken far guts, volt nit zein kain tseit tsu baklogen zich oif shlechts"

If we thanked God for the good things, there wouldn't be time to weep over the bad. (Yiddish Proverb)

The popular notion of meditating is that of an individual sitting on a mat, cross-legged (a very uncomfortable position for most of us), breathing in and out, eyes closed, surrounded by silence, or accompanied by the intonation of a chant or mantra, sitting for what seems to be an interminable length of time.

This description, while accurate, need not exhaust all meditative possibilities.

To cultivate an awareness of gratefulness, meditative moments, however brief, can have a nurturing impact and produce a cumulative capacity to call upon such feelings at various challenging times in one's life. The essential requirement is the continuous commitment to consciously incorporate a sense of gratefulness as a natural and inseparable part of our everyday experiences.

For those who are comfortable with a notion of God, you may express your gratefulness in the words—I THANK YOU.

For others, perhaps the phrase—I AM GRATEFUL FOR-would be more suitable.

Some additional meditation suggestions:

Morning: Upon awakening, at the first sign of awareness, recite "modeh ani", "I thank" or express in your own words or thoughts the idea of being thankful for being alive and awake.

Pay attention to any sounds you may hear, or simply to the silence.

I AM GRATEFUL FOR MY SENSE OF HEARING

Open your eyes slowly. Look around and take in what you see.

I AM GRATEFUL FOR WHAT I SEE.
BLESSED ARE YOU WHO OPENS THE EYES OF THOSE WHO CANNOT SEE.

Feel the warmth of the blanket, pillow or mattress.

I AM GRATEFUL FOR WHAT I FEEL.

Notice any aromas in the room or house-perhaps that of coffee brewing, or breakfast being made.

I THANK YOU FOR MY SENSE OF SMELL.

Getting out of bed, placing your feet on the floor, standing up, could elicit an awareness of the blessing that is contained in the sheer movement of one's body.

I BLESS YOU FOR RAISING UP THOSE WHO ARE BENT AND DOWNTRODDEN.

Before you go through your morning tasks, spend a few moments considering where you live. Look around and be attentive to the space that surrounds you-the walls that protect you, paintings and pictures that adorn these walls, the windows that lead outside to views of the sky, trees or your neighbor's brick wall, the bathroom with the facilities to ease your daily hygienic preparations, the kitchen with its modern appliances that make food preparation so efficient and convenient, focus on being given the gift of being able to fulfill all the tasks and chores necessary for the day.

While washing or brushing your teeth, consider the gifts of healthy teeth, clean water, scented soap filling your nose with pleasant fragrance and the ability to smell and feel the soft lather of the soap. Our bodies are the temples of our souls. As we wash, we are grateful for the cleanness and purity that we experience.

BLESSED ARE YOU . . . . WHO ORDAINED THE WASHING OF THE HANDS

After using the toilet, we may utter quietly or think the following words:

I PRAISE YOU—FOR HAVING CREATED BODILY ORIFICES THAT ALLOW ME TO ELIMINATE THAT WHICH MAY POISON MY BODY AND DO ME HARM.

While dressing, imagine those who don't have the variety of clothes you have at your disposal. In the winter, as we snuggle under our blankets or cover ourselves in fluffy sweaters and furry coats, to be clothed is a reason for gratefulness.

BLESSED ARE YOU WHO CLOTHES THE NAKED.

At breakfast, each item of food or beverage can be eaten or drunk slowly and mindfully, considering the complex process that lead to the availability of food on one's table. Try not to eat while engaged in another activity ie. last minute homework, office work, reading the newspaper or watching T.V.

BLESSED ARE YOU WHO BRINGS FORTH BREAD, FOOD, FROM THE EARTH

As we leave for work, school or become engaged in other errands or tasks, we may consider the gift of mobility.

BLESSED ARE YOU WHO GUIDES THE STEPS OF ALL LIVING CREATURES.

Afternoon: As the day progresses many are the moments when our minds are not connected to anything tangible or demanding in terms of work or other daily responsibilities; rather, we find ourselves driving a car, walking down the street, sitting on a subway or in a bus, when our minds simply and naturally wander, flitting from one thought to the next, as unconscious and uncontrollable as the process of breathing. These extended periods of aimless thought are wonderful opportunities to focus upon the myriad gifts of everything in our lives to help engender a greater sense of gratefulness. Gratefulness meditations for a few minutes or longer act as spiritual interceptors that can inject a quality of balance and reality into our everyday, hectic lives. Amidst our racing thoughts, many of which are often negative, numbing and self-defeating, a brief recess of gratefulness recognition can be extremely helpful.

As we devote our thoughts to plan, to aspire, to imagine the future, to review the past, anticipating and remembering, time is always available when we can stop and say "thank you."

If one is more formally religious, make use of prayer as a concentrated period of gratefulness awareness usually enumerated in the formal prayers of the prayer book.

Evening: At dinnertime, usually unrushed and more leisurely, the opportunity presents itself to introduce a dimension of grateful meditation related to eating and food. Jewish tradition ordains the reciting of blessings before and after the meal.

WE PRAISE YOU FOR BRINGING FORTH BREAD FROM THE EARTH. WE PRAISE YOU WHO GRACIOUSLY SUSTAINS THE WORLD WITH KINDNESS PROVIDING ALL CREATURES WITH FOOD.

Our thinking and feeling process, not only our behavior, become habituated by repetition. By deliberately and thoughtfully interjecting this constant consciousness of life as a gift, something that was given to us lovingly, we train our minds to perceive life gratefully, and thereby give ourselves greater happiness and well-being.

Formal Jewish Prayer as a meditative exercise in gratefulness

The Amidah prayer, the standing prayer that is regarded by Jewish tradition as the central prayer of the worship service, contains a series of petitions for the myriad blessings of life. I suggest that each of these requests is already available within the existing context of the world and human life, if not in actuality then in the realm of possibility and potential. Grateful awareness of these many gifts can spark and nurture the realization and fruition of these endowments and spiritual capacities. Some of the material has already been incorporated in the "Gratefulness practice" exercises following the earlier chapters.

BLESSED ARE YOU WHO GRACIOUSLY GRANTS US INTELLIGENCE.

We may feel that we are not smart enough. We may find ourselves comparing ourselves with others whom we consider to be more intelligent, cleverer, and more talented. As a result, we are beset by feelings of inferiority.

Focus on one thing that you are proud of that you achieved as a result of your own ability and intelligence. Consider being grateful for your own mind.

I AM GRATEFUL FOR MY ABILITY TO THINK
I AM GRATEFUL FOR MY TALENTS
I AM GRATEFUL FOR WHO I AM.

BLESSED ARE YOU WHO DESIRES THE EXERCISE OF OUR CAPACITY TO CHANGE.

Many feel that they fall short of what they can become and achieve, feeling stuck or paralyzed. The sense of powerlessness is not uncommon, and often we drift into ways of being and behaving over which we feel we have no control. We lose our sense of being able to choose and to change.

Think about one thing you were able to change in your life, however inconsequential it may appear. Remember your state of mind before the change and how You saw life after the change.

I AM GRATEFUL FOR THE OPPORTUNITY TO CHANGE
I AM GRATEFUL FOR THE DESIRE TO CHANGE
I AM GRATEFUL FOR THE STRENGTH TO CHANGE.

BLESSED ARE YOU HEALER OF ISRAEL

My body and spirit may be broken. Perhaps a loved one is now ill, in the hospital, at home convalescing, or at the final stages of life. I reach out to the source of healing in the universe and beyond. I turn to loved ones knowing I am not alone.

I AM GRATEFUL FOR MY HEALTH
I AM GRATEFUL FOR THE HEALTH OF MY LOVED ONES
I AM GRATEFUL FOR THOSE OF THE HEALTH PROFESSION WHO HEAL
I AM GRATEFUL FOR THE CONCERN AND ASSISTANCE OF THOSE WHO CARE.

WE PRAISE YOU FOR THE BOUNTY OF THE LAND.

How often do we take our prosperity for granted? While so many hunger for the basic necessities of survival, we have so much. In our gratefulness, we sense our compassion for the hungry of this world.

I THANK YOU FOR MY FOOD.
I AM GRATEFUL TO THOSE WHO BRING FOOD TO MY TABLE- THE FARMER, TRUCKER, GROCERY STORE OWNER, THE ONES WHO COOK MY FOOD.
I THANK YOU FOR THE PLEASURES OF FOOD AND DRINK

BLESS YOU WHO GATHERS THE DISPERSED OF OUR PEOPLE.

There are so many homeless men, women and children, dispersed everywhere, in far away refugee camps and on the streets of our own cities and towns. We have homes, places that give us safety and protection, roofs over our heads and walls that keep away the perils of the night. We consider ways of opening our homes to others.

I THANK YOU FOR MY HOME
I THANK YOU FOR WOOD, BRICK, STONE AND GLASS, THE BUILDING BLOCKS OF MY DWELLING PLACE
I THANK YOU FOR MY FAMILY AND ALL THOSE WHO MAKE MY HOUSE A HOME.

PRAISED ARE YOU WHO LOVES JUSTICE AND COMPASSION.

How incredible is the human desire for justice, for fairness and compassion! Think of one injustice committed against you, against a loved one, or against any one individual or group anywhere. Think of ways you can bring justice and compassion into your life, to make things a little fairer and more just.

I AM GRATEFUL FOR KNOWING WHAT IS RIGHT
I AM GRATEFUL FOR MY CONSCIENCE
I AM GRATEFUL FOR THE LAWS THAT HELP MAKE THIS A MORE JUST SOCIETY.

PRAISED ARE YOU WHO LISTENS TO PRAYER.

How precious it is to find a sympathetic ear, one who listens with understanding and acceptance to our words. To be listened to, to be paid attention to is a gift for which we are grateful.

How rewarding is it to listen to others with compassion and sensitivity. The art of listening is a true gift.
I AM GRATEFUL FOR THOSE WHO LISTEN WHEN I NEED THEM
I AM GRATEFUL FOR NOT BEING JUDGED TOO HARSHLY BY OTHERS.
I AM GRATEFUL FOR MY WILLINGNESS TO LISTEN ATTENTIVELY TO THOSE WHO NEED MY CARE AND CONCERN.

WE PRAISE YOU, THE SOURCE OF PEACE-SHALOM.

Think of war and its suffering victims. Consider the gift in being able to conceive of peace. Bring to your mind's eye a moment of peace in your own life and contemplate that moment. What can you do to bring peace?

I AM GRATEFUL FOR THE POSSIBILITY OF PEACE.
I AM THANKFUL FOR THOSE WHO SEEK PEACE AND PURSUE IT.
MAY WE ALL KNOW PEACE.

Repeat the syllables of—"SHA-LOM"—in your breathing. On the in-breath, we say-"SHA"—and on the out-breath we recite—"LOM." We can add-"MODEH"—"I THANK"-to the in-breath an—"SHALOM"—"PEACE"-to the out breath.

Why not?
In place of worry, why not welcome?
Instead of moping, why not marvel?
In lieu of abrogating, why not appreciating?
In place of misfortune, why not the miraculous?
Instead of appetite, why not amazement?
In lieu of grumbling, why not gratefulness?
Why not? Why Not?

ENDNOTES

1. Ruth Brin, *Harvest: Collected Poems and Prayers*; Reconstructionist Press, NY, 1986, p.156-58.
2. David Hume, *A Treatise of Human Nature*, in Raphael, D.D., ed.1969, *British Moralists 1650-1800, vol. 2*, Oxford University Press, p.16
3. Immanuel Kant, 1964/1797. *The Doctrine of Virtue, Part 2 of The Metaphysic of Morals*. Translated by Mary. McGregor, Phila. University of Pennsylvania Press
4. Emmons, R.A. & McCullough, M.E, The *Psychology of Gratitude*, Oxford University Press, 2004, p. v.
5. Kornfield, Jack, *After the Ecstasy the Laundry*, Bantam Books, 2000, p. 33.
6. *Deut.* 30:12-13
7. *Deut.* 30:13
8. Mary Oliver, *The Sun, New and Collected Poems*, Beacon Press, Boston, Mass.
9. M.R. Bennett and P.M.S Hacker's *Philosophical Foundations of Neuroscience*, p. 337, Malden, MA: Blackwell Publishing, 2003.
10. David Steindel-Rast in *Psychology of Gratitude*, Oxford, NY, p. 286-287.
11. Webster's New World Dictionary, William Collins Publishers, Cleveland, Ohio, 1979.
12. *Psalms* 115: 18
13. Alter, Robert, *The Book of Psalms, W.W. Norton &Company, 2007, p. xx*- "Again and again, the psalmists tell us that man's ultimate calling is to use the resources of human language to celebrate God's greatness and to express gratitude for His beneficent acts."
14. *Midrash Tehillim* 80:56
15. *Daily Prayer Book*
16. Ibid
17. *Deuteronomy* 28:45-47

18. Emmons, R.A. & McCullough, M.E. (Eds.) *The Psychology of Gratitude*, Oxford, NY, 2005, p.301-303.
19. Greene, Brian, *New York Times, Sunday Opinion*, Sunday, June 1, 2008, p.14
20. *Deut.* 11: 22.
21. *Psalms*, 13:6
22. Sexton, Anne, *The Complete Poems:Anne Sexton*, Boston, Houghton Mufflin, 1988, p.455
23. Launer, Schiff, & Lynn, 1992, *My Cousin Vinny*.
24. Wex Michael *Born to Kvetch*, St. Martin's Press, 2005, p. 1
25. Ibid. p. 2
26. *A Social and Religious History of the Jews*, vol.1, Columbia University Press, 1952, p. 297, note 7.
27. Oliver, Mary, *Red Bird*, Beacon Press, p. 30
28. Rabbi Harold Kushner, *The Lord is My Shepherd*, Anchor Books, 2003, p.151
29. Ibid.
30. *The New York Times, National, Sunday,* August 5, 2007.
31. *Ecclesiastes*, 5:9-10
32. *The Bhammadasad* translated by Ekanath Easwaran, Nilgri Press, 1985, pp. 355, 358.
33. *Ethics of the Fathers,* chapter. 4, 1.
34. Babylonian Talmud, *Berachot,* 10a
35. Soloveitchick, *The Festival of Freedom*, Ktav Publishing Co., NY, 2006, p. 114.
36. Kushner, Harold, *The Lord is My Shepherd,* Anchor Books, 2003, p. 151.
37. Sommers & Kosmitzki, "Emotion and Social Context: An American-German Comparison", *British Journal of Social Psychology,* 27 pp.35-49, 1988.
38. *The New York Times Magazine*-August 8, 2004
39. Joseph B. Soloveitchik, *The Lonely Man of Faith,* Doubleday, 1992, p.16
40. Chpt. 32:20
41. *Genesis,* 6:5
42. *Between God and Man,* The Free Press, NY, 1959, p.98
43. P.311
44. *Kitchen Table Wisdom,* Riverhead Books, NY, 1996 p.47
45. *The Lonely Man of Faith*, pp. 35-36.
46. Soloveitchik, J.B. *Out of the Whirlwind*, Ktav Publishing House, Inc. 2003, p.xix
47. *Siddur Beit Yaakov*, Lemberg, 1903, p. 42-Publ. Otzar Hasefarim, NY.
48. Agnon S.Y. *Kol Kitvei Agnon, vol. X, "Petichah L'Kaddish,"* 1959
49. Mishnah *Berachot* 9:2.
50. Talmud, *Berachot,* 60

51 Mary Sarton, in *Selected Poems of Mary Sarton*, W.W. Norton and Co.1978
52 Steindl-Rost, *Gratefulness, the Heart of Prayer*, Paulist Press, NY/Mahwah, NJ, p. 199.
53 Chpt. 42:5
54 New York Times, *Book review*, Sept. 12, 2004, p.31
55 *Man is not Alone*, p.58
56 Zilboorg, *Fear of Death*, Psychoanalytic Quarterly, 1943; 12; p.465-475 in Becker, Ernest, *The Denial of Death*, The Free Press, 1973, p.14.
58 Ibid
57 Becker, *Denial of Death*, p.21.
58 Bergson, Henri, *The Idea of Nothing*, in Creative Evolution, Modern Library, p. 323.
59 Khalil Gibran, *The Prophet*, Alfred A. Knopf, NY, 1923.
60 *The New Yorker*, Feb. 27, 2006
61 Ibid. John Lanchaster, p.78
62 Heschel, Abraham Joshua, *Man's Quest for God, Charles* Scribner's Sons, p.5.
63 Spirituality as I understand it can be defined as follows: "That which gives meaning, purpose and direction in life, is shared by others, incorporates the commitment to a transcendent value, is articulated in symbols, metaphors and images and promotes positive ethical behavior toward others."
64 Miner, P.S. (1962) Thanksgiving as a synthesis of the temporal and eternal. In H.A. Johnson & Thulstrup (Eds.), *A Kierkegaard critique* (pp 297-308), New York: Harper & Brothers.
65 *Man is Not Alone*, Farrar, Straus & Giroux, NY, 1951 p.138.
66 Quoted in *After the Ecstasy, the Laundry*, Bantam Books, 2000, p.213
67 Talmud, *Sanhedrin* 4:5
68 Soloveitchick, J.B. *The Lonely Man of Faith, p.24*
69 *Man is Not Alone*, pp.126-127.
70 *Orot ha-kodesh, Sacred Lights,* section 3:221
71 *Numbers* 15:39.
72 *Peace is Every Step*, Bantam Books, NY, 1992, p.33
73 *Daily Prayer Book*
74 Talmud *Pesachim* 87b
75 Alter, Robert, *The Book of Psalms, W.W.* Norton, 2007, p.xxviii
76 *Sloan-Kettering*, Schoken Books, NY, 2002 p.43
77 *Ethics of the Fathers*, Chpt 2:4
78 *Renew Our Days,* Rabbi Ronald Aigen, Montreal, 1996, p.354
79 NY Times, *Science Section*, Tues. Jan 11, 2005,pp.1-4
80 Soloveitchik, *Worship of the Heart*, Ktav, NY, 2003, pp.130-31

81 *Genesis* 34:1
82 See Talmud *Bava Batra* 16b-17a. The various forms of 'kol'-all-are associated with not only Abraham but with the other Patriarchs, Isaac and Jacob as well. The Bible tells us regarding Isaac: "I ate from everything-'mi-kol'" (Gen.27: 3). With regards to Jacob, we read: "I have everything-kol" Gen.33: 11) The Talmud then proceeds to point out its interpretation of 'everything'-kol suggesting that the Patriarchs enjoyed every possible blessing from God, even a taste of the World to Come. Yet we know that each patriarch suffered a great deal in his life. How could we understand their lives as perfectly blessed with everything? I would interpret this to mean that they all shared the unique spiritual capacity to be profoundly grateful which allowed them to experience the 'other worldly' quality of life, in spite of their many ordinary travails.
83 I am grateful to a colleague, Rabbi Phil Pohl, for this observation.
84 Fulghum, Robert, *All I Really Need To Know I Learned in Kindergarten,* Ballantine, NY, 2003, p.58
85 *Kitchen Table Wisdom,* p.93
86 P.293
87 *Renew our Days,* p.299
88 *Lamdeni,* Sifriat Poalim
89 *Daily Prayer Book*
90 B. Talmud, *Berachot* 59b
91 Jerusalem Talmud, *Berachot* 9:2,13b-c
92 *Midrash Aseret Hadibrot,* edited and compilrd with a literary critical commentary by Anat Shapira, p.29, The Bialik Institute, Jerusalem, 2005.
93 *Spiritual Literacy,* Frederic and Mary Ann Brussat, Scribner,1996, p.505
94 Seyyed Hossein Nasr, *The Heart of Islam-Enduring Values for Humanity,* HarperSanFransisco, 2002, P.9
95 Smith, Houston and Novak, Philip, *Buddhism, A Concise Introduction,* HarperSanFransisco, 2003, P.53
96 Conze, Edward, *Buddhism: Its Essence and Development, NYC,* Harper & Row, 1951, P.40
97 Thich Nhat Hanh, *No Death, No Fear,* Riverhead Books, NY, p. 41.
98 Ibid, p. IX
99 Streng, F.J., Introduction: Thanksgiving as a worldwide response to life, in J.B. Carman and F.J. Streng, Eds. *Spoken and Unspoken Thanks: Some Comparative Soundings,* Cambridge, MA, Harvard University Center for the Study of World Religions, p.1-9.
100 Heschel, Abraham Joshua, *God in Search of Man,* Harper Torchbooks edition, 1955, p.49

101. Dawkins, Richard, *The God Delusion*, Houghton Mifflin Co. Boston, NY 2006.
102. *Psychology of Gratitude,* p. 86
103. Klein, Melanie, *Envy and Gratitude, &Other Works, 1943-1963,* Delacorte Press, 1975, pp.187-189.
104. Susan Jacoby, *Freethinkers, a History of American Secularism*, Metropolitan Books, 2004,Appendix p. 369
105. *Pirkei Avot-Teachings of the Sages*: 1: 2
106. Oliver, Mary, Th*irst, Beacon Press, Boston, 2006,* p. 1
107. B. *Shabbat* 88b
108. Robert J. Landry, *God Lives in Glass*, Skylight Paths Publ. Woodstock, Vermont, 2001 p. 49.
109. *Genesis Rabbah* 6:5
110. In Idel, Moshe, *Absorbing Perfections-Kabbalah and Interpretation,* Yale University Press, 2002, pp. 425-426.
111. Quoted from *Mindfulness,* Ellen J. Langer, Perseus Press, Cambridge, MA, 1989, p.116
112. *Full Catastrophe Living,* Dell Publ. NY. pp. 442-443.
113. Beliefnet—*The Wisdom of Empty Minds*, 5/15/2001
114. *That's Funny-You Don't Look Buddhist,* Harper-San Fransisco, 1996, p.53.
115. *Exodus Rabbah* 24: 1
116. Walker, Alice, *The Color Purple,* Harcourt Brace Jovanovich, NY. 1982 p. 168
117. Ibid.
118. Psalms 24: 1
119. Tosafot Talmud, *Brachot* 4:1
120. Talmud, *Berachot* 58b
121. *Spiritual Literacy*, p.218
122. Mishneh Torah, *Hilchot Yesodei ha-Torah*, 2:2.
123. Oliver, Mary, *Thirst,* Beacon Press, Boston, 2006, p. 37.
124. P.77
125. *All I Need to Know I Learned in Kindergarten,* p.179
126. *Man's Quest for God,* Charles Scribner's Sons, NY, pp. 84, 85, 137.
127. Ibid p. 15
128. *Renew Our Days,* p. 3
129. *Kol Haneshama*-Prayerbook for the Days of Awe, The Reconstructionist Press, 1999, p. 239
130. B. Talmud, *Megillah,* 18a.
131. B. Talmud, *Megillah*, 31a
132. Kushner: *The Lord is My Shepherd*, p. 154

133. *Father of Life,* Language of Faith, ed. Nahum Glatzer, 1974, Schoken Books.
134. *Before,* Gates to the New City, ed. Howard Schwartz, 1983
135. Heschel, *I Asked for Wonder* p. ii.
136. Kunitz, Stanley with Lentine, Genine, *The Wild Braid,* W.W. Norton &Co., 2005
137. Heschel, *God in Search of Man,* p.290
138. *Chronicles* 16:29
139. B.Talmud, *Sotah* 14a—"Rabbi Simlai taught: The Torah begins with deeds of loving kindness and ends with deeds of loving kindness. It begins with deeds of loving kindness as it is written:' and the Lord made for Adam and his wife garments of skins and clothed them-Gen.3: 21. It ends with deeds of loving-kindness as it is written, "And He buried him (Moses) in the valley of the land of Moab"-Deut. 34:8."
140. Twersky,Isadore, *Some Aspects of the Jewish Attitude Toward the Welfare State,* Tradition, Vol. 5-No.2, Spring, 1963
141. *Sifre*, Deuterornomy, Ekev
142. B.Talmud *Sotah* 14a
143. *Spiritual Literacy*
144. Brother David Steindl Rost, *Gratefulness, the Heart of Prayer,* p. 176.
145. *Leviticus* 19:18
146. P.697
147. *Man is not Alone,* pp. 104-5
148. *A Path with Heart,* p.202
149. *Deut.*6: 5
150. *Etz Chayim, Rabbinical* Assembly, NY, 2000 note 5, p. 1025
151. *Leviticus* 19:34; Deut. 10:19
152. *Etz Chayim,* p. 700, note 34.
153. P.1123, note 8
154. NY Times, *Benedict Carey*, July, 2004
155. *Genesis* 1:28
156. B.Talmud *Kiddushin* 31a-b.
157. Ibid
158. *Spiritual Literacy*, pp.430-31
159. Ibid, p.440
160. *Man is Not Alone,* pp.64, 122.
161. *Judaism as a Civilization,* The Reconstructionist Press, NY 1957, p. 316.
162. Ibid.p.318
163. Mordechai M. Kaplan, *Communings of the Spirit,* edited by Mel Scult, Wayne University Press and The Reconstructionist Press, 2001.

164 *Deuteronomy* 30:19.
165 B.Talmud 54b
166 Thich Nhat Hanh, *Call Me by My True Names*, Prallax Press, Berkley, Calif.
167 Uzi Hitman, Israeli songwriter, *Todah*, Renew our Days, pp.301-302.

Made in the USA
Lexington, KY
28 June 2014